TEENAGERS
LEAVE A MARK

The Complete Guide to
Your Destiny and Dream

TROY BLAIN BORDEN

WESTBOW
PRESS®
A DIVISION OF THOMAS NELSON
& ZONDERVAN

Scriptures taken from the Holy Bible, New International Version®, NIV®. Copyright © 1973, 1978, 1984, 2011 by Biblica, Inc.™ Used by permission of Zondervan. All rights reserved worldwide. www.zondervan.com The "NIV" and "New International Version" are trademarks registered in the United States Patent and Trademark Office by Biblica, Inc.™ Scripture taken from the King James Version of the Bible

WestBow Press books may be ordered through booksellers or by contacting:

WestBow Press
A Division of Thomas Nelson & Zondervan
1663 Liberty Drive
Bloomington, IN 47403
www.westbowpress.com
1 (866) 928-1240

Because of the dynamic nature of the Internet, any web addresses or links contained in this book may have changed since publication and may no longer be valid. The views expressed in this work are solely those of the author and do not necessarily reflect the views of the publisher, and the publisher hereby disclaims any responsibility for them.

Any people depicted in stock imagery provided by Thinkstock are models, and such images are being used for illustrative purposes only. Certain stock imagery © Thinkstock.

ISBN: 978-1-5127-8671-2 (sc)
ISBN: 978-1-5127-8672-9 (hc)
ISBN: 978-1-5127-8670-5 (e)

Library of Congress Control Number: 2017907683

Print information available on the last page.

WestBow Press rev. date: 07/12/2017

Teenagers Leave a Mark is dedicated to my children—
Brandon, Molly, and Blain—and my grandchildren and
future great grandchildren, in hope that each one of them
will discover their destiny and pursue their dream.

Contents

PREFACE

You Have An Amazing Spirit

Someone in your generation needs to know God and you are the perfect person for the job. You have an amazing spirit. If you haven't already done so, it's time for you to begin a close friendship with God. He knows you better than anyone else. He's trying hard to get your attention because he wants you to begin a friendship with him. God is an awesome person who will enable you to have a great life. With God, you will literally never be alone. He'll enable you to rise above trouble and help you become the person you really want to be. But first you must invite him to participate in your life. Then you can get to know him even better.

Jesus addressed a problem that everyone faces: you're *immortal*, yet *imperfect*. After your body dies, your spirit and personality will continue to live on for eternity. Ideally, you would exist with God in heaven. But you can't. Even though the universe God created doesn't appear to be perfect, God *is* perfect; and the problem is ... you're not. So you cannot live with God. It's the greatest of all your problems: you're immortal, yet imperfect, so you're doomed to live for eternity in hell—far away from God.

If you could be made to be perfect (at least in the eyes of God), then you could spend eternity in heaven with God after you die. Jesus made it possible.

Jesus was unlike anyone else in the way he lived his life because it was a perfect life. Still, when he was about thirty-three years old, during flawed legal proceedings he was found to be a person who behaved in many ways that were unacceptable to God. Then he was given a punishment reserved only for the worst of sinners: death on a cross.

Knowing that Jesus didn't ever do anything he wasn't supposed to do, God raised him from the dead after three days, as Jesus predicted he would. So God demonstrated in a clear way to everyone that Jesus did not deserve the judgment he was given and that he did not deserve to die.

After the resurrection Jesus was seen by or met with more than five hundred people. All Roman and Jewish historians of the time wrote about the event—it was big news! The resurrection proved that Jesus did not deserve to be punished. Then God took Jesus directly to heaven, demonstrating yet again that Jesus had lived a life that was perfect and that he was then able to live with God.

Then what about Jesus's death? Since he didn't deserve the punishment he received, he left you with a way to go to heaven. Here's how it works. You don't have to wait until you die to face God. You can pray to God right now and reason with him, saying, "I want today to be considered the day I die and see you face-to-face in eternity."

You can say to God, "I understand that you're perfect, and I'm not. I know I cannot exist with you in eternity and there is only one other place for me to exist after I die. That's a legitimate judgment in light of the circumstances." Then you can ask that arrangements be made on your behalf. Say something such as this: "God, Jesus was separated from you even though he did not deserve to be. Will you accept his death and separation in place of my own?"

Since Jesus's death was a sacrifice he willingly made and since it was a penalty God knew he didn't owe, if you ask God to accept Jesus's punishment and separation as a substitute for your own, God will do so as long as arrangements are made before you die. On whatever day that happens, God considers it to be the day you die. The way God sees it, you stood before him, understood and accepted your judgment, and then you were separated from God for all eternity. But in reality Jesus was separated from God on your behalf and you're still alive.

When you really do die there is no penalty left for you to pay. You were already judged for being imperfect, for doing what you knew you were not supposed to do (for sinning). Then in God's eyes you were punished. Afterward you begin a new kind of life, a life in which you won't be judged like that again because there's nothing left to judge.

Since you no longer deserve to be judged for having done what you knew you were not supposed to do, it's like you never did it. There is no longer the threat that imperfection will separate you from God in the afterlife. There is no longer anything separating you from God in this life either. Your circumstances are different now and your spirit is also different. To guarantee that you will indeed experience eternal life in heaven, your spirit is given a small deposit of eternal life right away—a kind of life it never had before. This is the same kind of eternal life that you will experience in heaven.

Scripture says your spirit is "quickened" or made alive.[1] It now has the ability to communicate with God, Spirit to spirit, unhindered as if you were in heaven. The Spirit of God and your spirit communicate best when you're reading the Bible and praying. These are moments of clarity. When you pray to God you're spending time with "the God of hope."[2] Likewise, when you read your Bible you will discover that "everything that was written in the past was written to teach us, so that through the endurance taught in the scriptures and the encouragement they provide we might have hope."[3]

Your intuition, conscience, and hope ought to be noticeably clearer. You should realize as never before that God wants to get to know you better. Even though mortality still holds you apart, God wants to hear what you think, how you feel, your hopes and dreams, your problems and concerns.

Going to heaven is ultimately about a friendship you're beginning with God, a friendship that will last forever. Being baptized is a way of taking action to build this friendship. Baptism is a way for you to demonstrate to the world exactly what you're hoping for. During baptism you're dunked under water to symbolize your death, burial, and judgment. Then you're pulled up out of the water to show that, despite being buried, you're still alive. Only it's a new kind of life in which you won't be required to endure a judgment like that again.

You now have the opportunity to enjoy a great friendship with God and friendships with other Christian teenagers. Find a church you feel good about, with people you fit in with. God's plan is that together with other teenagers you'll discover that any of your needs and weaknesses can be turned into assets and strengths, with God's help—just as God helped you rise above the fact that you're immortal, yet imperfect. You'll find that your biggest needs and weaknesses are always the seeds of God's most powerful works in your life!

The apostle Paul was capable of dealing with needs and weaknesses in his own way, but instead he wanted God's power to be revealed in his life. God had explained to him that "my power is made perfect in weakness."[4] So Paul didn't mind being weak. He chose to embrace weakness and rely on God. Paul said, "I will boast all the more gladly about my weaknesses, so that Christ's power may rest on me. That is why, for Christ's sake, I delight in weaknesses, in insults, in hardships, in persecutions, in difficulties. For when I am weak, then I am strong."[5]

Even Jesus subjected himself to weakness so he could become a high priest who could empathize with your weakness. Scripture explains that "we do not have a high priest who is unable to empathize with our weaknesses, but we have one who has been tempted in every way, just as we are."[6] Jesus understands needs and weaknesses. When he was physically among us, his strategy was to change the world by entrusting his message to a small group of disciples who were very weak politically, economically, and even religiously. Then God gave them the Holy Spirit to help them in their weakness and in the power of the Holy Spirit they literally changed the world. Today it's still true: "the Spirit helps us in our weakness."[7]

God wants you to experience a great sense of happiness and a richness to life in the same way. Not by your own power—by God's power! So you can see why your greatest need or weakness is actually the seed of God's most powerful work in your life. God wants to achieve amazing things right now, in you and through you. Things that will require the kind of power that he can only show in your weakness. As you pursue your dream you will recognize that no matter what your need or weakness, God is helping you in powerful ways as you grow more reliant upon him. That will make you more hopeful than ever before about achieving your dream and fulfilling your destiny.

Preparing For A Dream

Do you have a lifelong dream? Is it well defined and written down? Does pursuing it give your life purpose? Experts speculate that only 3 percent of Americans have a dream they have written down. This number is surprisingly low considering the dynamic role a dream can play in your life. You'll improve your life dramatically and change the world in amazing ways by pursing a dream.

Martin Luther King Jr. captivated an entire nation by declaring, "I have a dream!"[8] Those four words are full of potential, yet rarely spoken. Two years after declaring his dream King witnessed the Civil Rights Act of 1964 and became the youngest person ever to receive the Nobel Peace Prize—all because of his dream.

Do you ever wonder about your purpose in life or your destiny? If you have ever asked for advice about what you should do with your life, in response you were probably asked what you were good at. Then you were encouraged to do whatever that was. This advice is confusing because it's great advice for establishing your goals but not for identifying your destiny. Yet the advice is usually the same whether you ask a parent, professor, pastor, or priest. You're left to speculate that there may be more to life than goals, but you are at a loss for where to turn for answers.

Pursuing a dream and fulfilling your destiny doesn't mean doing more of what you are already good at. Instead—and it's critically important for you to understand—pursuing a dream means finally becoming the person you've always wanted to be. The dream that will enable you to fulfill your destiny is not a type of goal. Goals come from your strengths. Goals represent wants and desires that you try to obtain with your natural talents, learned abilities, gifts, and ambitions. A dream is different because it comes from a predominant need or weakness that keeps pushing you until you finally begin pushing back. Your dream is designed to confront the shortcoming that plagues you most. A dream challenges you to excel where you are most vulnerable. You never begin with the strength you need to achieve your dream. But if you embrace it anyway, you will learn how to grow in new ways, depend on God, and develop as an individual. It's a fact of life. However, it's not presented as a guide for living in many sources other than *Teenagers Leave a Mark*.

A voice from somewhere inside tells you that even though you might feel insecure or incapable, you can actually achieve an extraordinary dream once you decide to face your most predominant need or weakness. The voice you hear is not meant to make you feel uncomfortable with yourself. Instead it holds out a promise, a clue that will guide you to something you ought to be searching for: a better life.

As an infant Helen Keller contracted a deadly illness that left her deaf, blind, and mute. When Helen was seven years old Ann Sullivan began teaching her to communicate. Once she began communicating Helen developed an insatiable appetite for learning. She eventually became the first deaf-blind person to graduate from college. Helen realized that her destiny was that the thing she was the worst at (communicating with others) would become what she was best at. She became a world-famous speaker and prolific author, who said, "I long to accomplish a great and noble task, but it is my chief duty to accomplish humble tasks as though they were great and noble. The world is moving along, not only by the mighty shoves of its heroes, but also by the aggregate of the tiny pushes of each honest worker."[9]

Pursuing a dream is not a great or noble task. Instead it's a humble task that produces a great and noble life—a life that's full of meaning and purpose. You're about to discover that having a dream is not so difficult. In fact, pursuing your dream will prove to be one of the most enjoyable and meaningful experiences of your life!

PART I

Creating A Dream

CHAPTER

Discover Your Purpose

Jordan invited his best friend, Robbie, over one day and Robbie brought his little sister, Kalli, along with him. It was cold out that day, so most of their time was spent hanging out in Jordan's room. A few weeks later Kalli went to see *Sesame Street Live* with her aunt and on the way home they were involved in a multicar pileup. Kalli sustained life-threatening injuries and had to be rushed to Nationwide Children's Hospital for emergency surgery. People were crying and praying throughout the waiting room when the doctor came out to deliver the awful news—the precious little girl they loved so much had not survived.

The unbelievable pain was still being felt months later when Robbie blurted out an unexpected confession to Jordan's mom. He said, "The last time we were at your house in Jordan's room, we opened a bag of Cheetos and got them all over our hands. Kalli was trying to jump as high as she could on Jordan's bed and when she finally got high enough she reached up and put her hand on the ceiling."

Then Jordan explained, "It's true, Mom. We didn't tell you because we didn't want you to wash it off." Each morning when he woke up Jordan had been looking up at the ceiling over his bed to see the Cheetos handprint of a special little girl he would never forget. Jordan and Robbie wanted to forever remember the fun they had with Kalli that day.

You might assume you will have the greatest impact on the world around you through your daily pursuits—your appearance, reputation, money, work, and education. However, even though these pursuits are necessary for a happy and productive life, they don't accurately or completely define who you are as a person. Like Kalli you are more likely to leave a mark while you're having fun, sharing your thoughts and emotions, expressing what's in your spirit, or simply being who you are as a person.

Your dream enables you to leave a mark by enhancing and developing your thoughts, emotions, and spirituality. In doing so, a dream also enables you to have more control over your life, giving you the sense that your life can be anything you want it to be. If you're honest with yourself you might admit that your appearance, reputation, money, work, and education haven't necessarily enabled you to become the person you really want to be. Despite the shortfalls, these daily pursuits are still good because they enable you to be productive.

Teenagers Leave a Mark is an opportunity to confidently face your most predominant need or weakness while at the same time developing your untapped mental, emotional, and spiritual potential; to live outside the box and challenge yourself to build a better life and a better friendship with God. This is your opportunity to design and pursue a dream that will add meaning and purpose to your life. You will come to discover that you are more than capable of mastering the area of life that is troubling you the most, no matter what it is.

The Old Testament explains that "when God created mankind, he made them in the likeness of God."[10] Like God your thoughts, emotions, and spirit are entirely unique to you. If you were given an assignment to record all that happened within your thoughts, emotions, and spirit for just one minute and then to communicate that to another person so effectively that they could duplicate that same one minute within themselves, you would never be able to do it. So much happens within you to such a degree that you're not capable of recording it or accurately communicating it to others—not even for a minute. You can never be duplicated and you forever remain fully known only to God.

At one time, only God possessed the ability to be a truly unique person. However, after great consideration God decided to share this special characteristic with human beings such as you and me. So the fact that you're unique is significant because the ability to be unique came from God. Be careful not to search for your life's purpose in ordinary daily pursuits. Instead discover it in the expression of your own unique thoughts, emotions, and spirit.

The first step toward pursing a dream is simply discovering that your purpose in life is not just to lead a productive existence. Your purpose in life is to think, feel, and express your spirit in unique ways. In other words, you shouldn't live to go to school and work. You go to school and work in order to get what you need to live. The same is true of your appearance, reputation, and money. These attributes should enhance your life, not suck the life out of you. This realization changes ordinary teenagers into extraordinary dreamers.

You are an ordinary teenager only to the extent that you go through life never pursuing a dream. You become an extraordinary dreamer once you begin searching and realize that you can actually become the person you really want to be. You're bound to achieve your dream because your thoughts are free to be industrious and inventive; your emotions are free to be curious and creative; your spirit is free to be intuitive and conscientious.

So relax and enjoy. Take some time to personally design your own dream—the dream that will enable you to fulfill your destiny and become an extraordinary teenager. The idea that you have a destiny and dream, and that you're about to discover what they are, is the beginning of a turning point in your life. It means you will become part of a group of teenagers who all share the same idea—God's idea. You're fortunate to be the keeper of this idea at this exact moment in history. You're inheriting two thousand years of progress toward one of the best ideas of Christianity, which is the largest and most diversified spiritual movement ever to span the globe. The spirit of this idea has now come to you and your generation, and you will see its very greatest days!

Define Your Destiny

One of the most interesting aspects of pursuing a dream is deciding what it should be. You may have already had opportunities in life to achieve your dream and fulfill your destiny. But you may not have recognized these opportunities because you didn't know what your dream was. These missed opportunities will continue to occur unless you take the time to discover your destiny and design a dream that will enable you to fulfill it.

You must have goals in order to lead a happy and productive life, but you absolutely must have a dream too; and you need to be motivated about both. This represents a healthy and balanced approach to life. While your goals spring from your strengths, your dream springs from your weakness. You use goals to help *ensure* your success in areas of life where success is critical. On the other hand, you use your dream to *hope for* success in an area of life that makes you feel weak or fearful.

Everyone has special talents, abilities, and gifts. It's not that you're the very best at what you do, but there are certain activities you enjoy and are good at. You are born with specific talents, you learn new abilities as you grow, and God gives you more gifts when you begin a friendship with him. God has given you these talents, abilities, and gifts to make it easier for you to accomplish your individual and group goals, and God helps you to make the most of them. Yet you cannot go through life investing everything you are in your goals, developing only the talents, abilities, and gifts you already possess. You also need to put some of your time and effort into a dream that will challenge you where you are weak and needy.

God has a uniquely perfect personality because he is the only uncreated being. It's the only weakness, of sorts, God has ever experienced. What if you were the only perfect person and you knew it? Wouldn't that affect your attitude? How would you behave toward others? Instead of using perfection as an excuse to be self-serving, God chose to do just the opposite and be generous toward others. In fact, that became God's dream—to give. He gave you life, the ability to be unique, creation to enjoy, his only Son, his Spirit, and his commitment to be with you forever. Even though God doesn't technically have a weakness, his dream has enabled him to turn this potential weakness into a strength, and in doing so to fulfill his destiny.

The dream that necessity dictates is the dream that will enable you to fulfill your own destiny, as God demonstrated. Deep within your own unique personality you have been programmed to excel in certain areas and to be lacking in others. Just as you can become an expert in the area of life in which you naturally excel, you can also become an expert in the area in which you are lacking the most. This area of your life is where you will discover your destiny. Rick

8

Warren, author of the best-selling book *The Purpose-Driven Life*, said, "We are fragile and flawed and break easily. But God will use us if we allow him to work through our weaknesses ... Instead of living in denial or making excuses, take the time to identify your weaknesses."[11]

Among the many heroes of faith mentioned in the New Testament book of Hebrews is Moses, who acknowledged, "I am slow of speech."[12] Gideon admitted, "My clan is the weakest in Manasseh and I am the least in my family."[13] Rahab confessed, "Our hearts melted and everyone's courage failed."[14] Necessity dictated that these three face their needs and weaknesses. In doing so they discovered their destinies as well as dreams that would enable them to fulfill their destinies. Each one's experience was the same: their "weakness was turned to strength."[15] Moses became a great leader and public speaker. Gideon turned out to be a brilliant military leader and strategist. Rahab single-handedly rescued several Israelite spies from the king of Jericho while saving her entire family from certain destruction.

Like the others, Rahab changed history simply by addressing her weakness in a positive way. After escaping Jericho she married one of the spies she had rescued and had a son named Boaz, who helped Ruth escape a world of poverty. After Boaz married Ruth, thirty-two generations later Rahab had a descendant named Jesus who helped the Jewish people escape a world of religious traditions that kept them far away from God.

What is your destiny? Almost any area of life can qualify as the subject of your destiny: your lifestyle, friendships, hobbies, personal history, or current circumstances. Your ordinary daily pursuits qualify too. Appearance, reputation, money, work, or education can be the subject of your destiny as long as you have a legitimate need or personal weakness in one of these areas. Obviously an addiction to drugs or alcohol can be the focus of your destiny. Even a personal ambition can be the subject of your destiny if circumstances in your life have left you with a need or weakness in this area.

Your most predominant need or weakness is easy to face with a dream. It's not a characteristic you chose for yourself and it doesn't define you. You may have been born with a handicap, personality quirk, medical dependency, genetic disposition toward addiction, or one of many other negative family traits. A need or weakness may have developed over time, such as a physical, mental, or emotional challenge; habit; fear; shame; guilt; stress; or simply a persistent, heartfelt desire or longing.

You may find it challenging to identify your most predominant need or weakness, especially if you are used to ignoring it. Keep in mind that you don't have to deal with it directly in a life-changing way. You simply need to identify what it is and what area of life it's in. Your destiny is hidden within that need or weakness just waiting to be discovered.

You may already have an idea of what your destiny might be. Nevertheless you will want to be certain that it's actually the result of a legitimate need or personal weakness. If you already believe you know what your destiny is, it's most likely because of a deep need of some sort. Set aside a few minutes to answer the following questions. They're designed to help you identify your own needs and weaknesses. In the following chapter you will use these answers to focus in on one area of your life. Then you will be able to design a dream that will enable you to fulfill your destiny. You are a complex person made up of many layers, so you will not be able to identify *all* of your needs and weaknesses. That's okay. Just do your best to identify your most predominant. It is finally time to discover your destiny!

Are you comfortable thinking about your needs and weaknesses?

_____

_____

Do you think identifying them now might lead to overcoming them or managing them better?

_____

_____

Does that make you more comfortable thinking about them?

_____

_____

How often do needs or weaknesses affect your life?

_____

_____

How many of your needs and weaknesses are within your control?

_____

_____

Do you believe you have a legitimate need? What do you think it is?

Example: It could be a persistent heartfelt desire, personal challenge, longing, or failed resolution.

_____

_____

What have you always felt a need for? Or what do you think a person with your personality needs in order to really enjoy life?

_____

_____

Do you believe you have a personal weaknesses? What do you think it is?

Example: You may have a personality quirk, habit, medical dependency, fear, shame, guilt, stress, genetic disposition toward an addiction, negative family trait, handicap, or physical, mental, or emotional challenge.

_____

_____

What is the weakness in your life that you make excuses for? Or what weakness has led you to make poor choices that caused you pain, grief, or regret?

_____

_____

Review your answers to the previous questions and identify the deepest, most hidden need or weakness, or the single most urgent need or weakness you're experiencing in your life right now.

_____

_____

It's your destiny to learn to be strong where you are weak and rich in the area of your life in which you have need. That will present more of a challenge for some than for others. After all, even though you can always improve as an individual, you cannot always change certain needs or weaknesses such as a disease, a handicap, or even a persistent heartfelt desire. That's okay, because you can still learn to be strong and lead a rich life. Pursuing the dream that will fulfill your destiny is the best way to do it. No matter what your need or weakness, with God's help you will discover how to master it with a dream.

In some ways God is like a master watchmaker and you are a tiny piece of a fine watch. At first you might wonder why God created you as a weak and fragile piece that is different from all the other pieces. Yet something incredible will happen when you accept who you are and what your destiny is. You will be joined together with other weak and fragile pieces in a way that only the master watchmaker can orchestrate. As unique pieces get joined together with other unique pieces, eventually something amazing will happen. A *tick* will be heard where it has never been heard before—then another and another.

Only then will you discover why you were created to be weak and fragile, and why you were placed close together with other weak and fragile teenagers. As you begin to move in a synchronized motion with other teenagers you will witness Christianity tick in ways it never has before and you will understand what the master has been working on. Then, more than ever before, you will be glad that you pursued the dream that enabled you to fulfill your destiny. You will finally become the person you really want to be while getting to know God better in the process and unexpectedly becoming a part of something much bigger than yourself.

CHAPTER

Design Your Dream

It's time to begin designing your dream. God has given you a unique destiny. Now God needs you to take it upon yourself to design your own dream and determine what you can do in order to pursue it. Begin by choosing one of three general categories that your dream will fit into. Will it be an *urgent* dream, a *personal* dream, or a *lifelong* dream?

Did you know that Jesus has a dream that fits into the *lifelong* dream category? The night he was betrayed Jesus prayed in the garden at Gethsemane, "Father, I want those you have given me to be where I am, and to see my glory."[16] Jesus didn't tell his Father "I want" because he was in need the way you think of your own needs. Instead Jesus was expressing his destiny. He has always desired to have close friendships with ordinary people like us because he sees you and me as significant and unique. What an opportunity it is for you to be invited to live with Jesus in a place where you can get to know him on a more personal level.

On one rare occasion Jesus took Peter, James, and John into the mountains so they could see him transfigured into how he will appear in heaven. Scripture says that "his face shone like the sun, and his clothes became as white as the light. Just then there appeared before them Moses and Elijah, talking with Jesus."[17] Moses and Elijah weren't there so Jesus could ask them for advice. Even though they had passed into eternity, they were still the same Moses and Elijah, and Jesus simply enjoyed talking with them. This experience demonstrated to Peter, James, and John that in addition to Jesus's face shining like the sun, he will also be just as social in heaven as he was on earth. Friendships that continue into eternity are what Jesus needs in his own unique way. So his destiny is to have friendships with you and me. A lifelong dream will enable him to achieve this destiny.

The following questions will help you determine where you are right now with your own individual destiny and into which general category your dream will fit. Set aside a few minutes to write down answers to the following questions. Try not to overanalyze the questions; answer them as quickly as possible. Don't answer them in terms of right or wrong, good or bad, success or failure. It's natural for you to think in these terms, but at this point all you need to do is answer the questions in an objective manner—nothing more.

What single area of your life is most negatively affected right now by a need or weakness?

Example: It may be your lifestyle, friendship, hobby, personal history, current circumstances, appearance, reputation, money, work, education, physical asset, or personal ambition.

_____

_____

How would your life change if you could unlock your potential and fulfill your destiny in this area of your life?

_____

_____

What poor choices have you made in the past regarding this area of your life?

_____

_____

How have you tended to avoid personal responsibility regarding this area of your life? What excuses have you made?

_____

_____

In what ways have you tried to be honest with yourself about this area of your life?

_____

_____

Do you think that it helped when you tried to be honest about it?

_____

_____

Are you in distress about this area of your life?

_____

_____

If you're not in distress, how critical is it that you address this area of your life? Is it important to you or optional?

_____

_____

You may be in distress because a certain area of your life is causing you real mental suffering, not just stress. Or you may be experiencing a lack of basic necessities that is more than just a passing difficulty, or physical pain that goes beyond discomfort. If so, then you're probably desperate for an *urgent* dream to bring stability back to your life as quickly as possible, because a need or weakness is overwhelming you.

On the other hand, you may be familiar with your need or weakness and are comfortable dealing with it at a casual pace. If so, a *personal* dream is enough to challenge your sense of adventure and creativity. You require a dream that will give you direction and help you develop your potential in a difficult but manageable area of life.

Finally, a *lifelong* dream is for you if you are strong and successful and you think you don't have a predominant need or weakness. You require a dream that will force you to uncover a hidden need or weakness. This kind of dream is designed to give purpose to your entire life and meaning to your very existence. After all, the deeper you have to dig to find a need or weakness, the more challenging your dream will be, the longer it will take you to achieve it, and the more deeply fulfilling it will be. A lifelong dream won't necessarily take a lifetime to achieve; it will simply require more time.

Identifying a dream isn't nearly as difficult as it might sound. In fact, you're going to identify several possible dreams. It will be an enjoyable experience. You know what area of life you want to focus on. Now you must simply think of a dream whose time has come.

Throughout life it's best to pursue a handful of dreams at the same time, not just one. You ought to have a lifelong dream to pursue for the long term while pursuing one or more personal dreams that give your life direction, and an urgent dream whenever a crisis arises. Even though it's ideal to pursue more than one at a time, you're only going to focus on one dream for the purpose of *Teenagers Leave a Mark* since you are still getting started and learning how to do it.

Try to think of a dream that is so challenging that, in order to achieve it, your need will have to become an asset or your weakness a strength. Try to think of a dream that is comfortable and also appealing to your sense of adventure and creativity. Believe there are always answers. Think of a dream that will force you to ask more questions than it answers. A dream like that might reveal God's purpose for your very existence.

A dream shouldn't be described in negative terms, as something you will stop doing or a way you will try to stop acting. Keep it positive. Also, a dream shouldn't be too far out of your league. Of course they all seem somewhat out of reach in the beginning, and they should.

It's now time to identify three or more possible dreams. You should write down anything that's challenging enough to make you confront your need or weakness in a positive way. John Whitmore of *Performance Consultants* says the purpose "is not to find the right answer but to create and list as many alternative courses of action as possible. The quantity of options is more important at this stage than the quality and feasibility of each one. When you're sure that you have no more ideas, just come up with one more."[18] If a dream doesn't seem motivating or seems too impractical, you can weed it out later.

Take a moment right now and brainstorm. Try to think of as many possible dreams as you can. Remember that you're not looking for goals. Goals are what you simply *want* to do. You are trying to identify possible dreams. Dreams are what you not only want to do but also *need* to do for very good reasons. Each dream you think of must be so challenging that the only way you will be able to achieve it is if you can become strong where you are weak or rich in the area of life where you currently have a need. Here are some questions that will help to stimulate ideas for possible dreams.

At the beginning of the chapter, what area of life did you decide to focus on?

_____

_____

How critical is it that you address this area of your life: are you in distress about it, is it important, or is it optional?

_____

_____

Is your dream an urgent dream (you're in distress about it), a personal dream (it's important to you), or a lifelong dream (it's optional as to whether or not you have to deal with it)?

_____

_____

In Chapter Two, what specific need or weakness did you decide to overcome with a dream?

_____

_____

What dream would be so challenging that in order to achieve it, your need would have to become an asset or your weakness become a strength?

_____

_____

What if you knew the perfect dream for you? What would it be?

_____

_____

What would your dream be if you had enough money to accomplish anything?

_____

_____

What would it be if you had all the help you needed?

_____

_____

What would it be if you could have a college degree in any subject?

_____

_____

What if any major obstacle could be made to disappear? What would your dream be then?

_____

_____

What if your past could be made to disappear and all your memories be pleasant? What would your dream be then?

_____

_____

What if you could change yourself into the ideal you, the perfect you? What would your dream be then?

_____

_____

Can you come up with just one more amazing dream that would be especially fun, make your life more complete, and still be so challenging that in order to achieve it your need would have to become an asset or your weakness become a strength?

_____

_____

You want to be sure you're going to get the maximum amount of pleasure from the dream you choose to pursue. Any one of your potential dreams is enough to fulfill your destiny. Pursue the one that will grant you the greatest sense of accomplishment—the dream that's exactly right for you. That way when your dream happens it will be more than an accomplishment. It will be a fantastic experience!

Helen Keller once said, "Many have a wrong idea of what constitutes real happiness. It is not obtained through self-gratification, but through fidelity to a worthy purpose."[19] Helen never experienced the pleasures of sight or sound, yet she led an exceptional life. Despite what you might think, happiness doesn't come from what you touch, taste, see, and hear. Instead of being the result of pleasure, true happiness is a richness to life that comes from your commitment to a worthy purpose, such as your own unique dream. It's a result of the growth of your thoughts, emotions, and spirit as you pursue the dream that will enable you to fulfill your destiny.

You must use your best judgment to make sure you're investing your time in the dream that's right for you. You do that by using your imagination to figure out which dream will make you happiest in the end. Samuel Clemens (Mark Twain) became a printer's apprentice at age twelve and a printer in New York City when he was just eighteen. Years later he left to become a riverboat pilot, where he remained until the start of the Civil War. Afterward he was a militiaman, miner, journalist, traveler, and lecturer. Clemens loved to write about his adventures. He wrote that "you can't depend on your judgment when your imagination is out of focus."[20] The way to judge which of your potential dreams will bring you the most happiness is by imagining each of them turning out perfectly. Then you will be able to determine which dream will be the most rewarding.

Jesus must have imagined his own dream turning out perfectly. When Jesus was betrayed by Judas Iscariot, he prayed, "Father, the hour has come. Glorify your Son, that your Son may glorify you."[21] In some sense, when Jesus prayed for glory he was praying for everything to turn out perfectly. He undoubtedly imagined the billions of fascinating friendships he would be able to have with ordinary people like us and how very happy that would make him. Scripture explains that "for the joy set before him he endured the cross."[22]

Take a moment to think of an example from your own life of a situation that turned out perfect in the end. Think of a time in your life when circumstances were a little scary. You bit the bullet and attempted to make it work. Much to your surprise, everything worked out and afterward you thought about how much better the situation turned out than you expected.

Perfection is a real possibility. Don't imagine the worst outcome; imagine the best! When you imagine your dream turning out perfectly, it becomes that much easier for you to pursue. Without realizing it you begin to unconsciously look for opportunities to make your dream happen just the way you imagined. Because once you have seen your dream turn out perfectly, then you really believe in it, even if you only saw it in your imagination. Albert Einstein once said, "Imagination is more important than knowledge. Knowledge is limited. Imagination encircles the world."[23]

The following questions are designed to help you imagine each one of your potential dreams turning out perfectly. Then you can decide which dream will bring you the most happiness. In a future chapter you will address whether or not the dream you chose is possible. Remember that "God gives wisdom, knowledge and happiness."[24] You must assume that with God's help all of your potential dreams are possible. Answer the following questions separately for each potential dream.

What is the advantage or disadvantage of the dream?

_____

_____

How do you imagine the dream will play out? What will circumstances be like?

_____

_____

How will the dream benefit others as well as yourself?

_____

_____

What will your life be like after achieving the dream?

_____

_____

On a scale from one to ten, how much happiness do you imagine the dream will bring you?

_____

_____

Could several dreams be blended to form a single dream? What exactly would the blended dream be?

_____

_____

Out of all of your possible dreams, which one are you going to pursue?

_____

_____

CHAPTER

Who Says It's Not Possible?

Up to this point your dream has existed only within your own mind and spirit. It would be great if you could discover your dream plus the ability to make it happen all within your mind and spirit. However, a tangible dream must be created in a tangible way: outside of yourself in the real world. To make that happen you must be willing to accept certain facts that can help you turn your dream into a reality.

When you're just beginning to drive and you're in an unfamiliar area and cannot find your way, it's easy to assume that someone gave you bad directions, the map is wrong, or signs are wrong. Later on when you figure out where you messed up, you can easily see which piece of information you misunderstood or failed to notice.

Your dream is not so different. Instead of trying to blame the facts after you fail, why not make those facts your allies before you begin. You can choose to not pay attention to the facts if you want to. After all, they exist outside of your mind and spirit, away from the ideas you have about your dream. Yet, gaining an understanding of the facts always helps you achieve your dream, even if the facts seem out of your control or appear to make your dream harder to achieve.

Jesus's dream required an investigation into the facts. According to scripture God is perfect even though the universe God created, as you and I understand it, may not appear to be. On the other hand you are not perfect, even though you understand yourself to be basically good. Your spirit and personality will continue to exist for eternity even after your body passes away. Jesus's dream is for you to be able to live where he is in eternity. However, you are imperfect and cannot coexist with a perfect God. So Jesus couldn't possibly hope for you to be with him in eternity after you die. This fact posed a serious problem for Jesus, yet he was determined to deal with it in a positive way.

The facts are pertinent to your success, not a subject to be avoided. Scripture explains that "true worshipers will worship the Father in the Spirit and in truth, for they are the kind of worshipers the Father seeks."[25] Pursuing your dream is one way to worship God, and he wants you to maintain a balance between your heart and the tangible world while you're doing it.

If you are willing to understand what impact the facts will have on your dream, then you will be more in control. That's important because if you are not in control of your dream you won't feel like pursuing it. This is especially true as you run into challenges because you will assume the outcome is out of your control. But that is not the case. You can help to control the outcome of your dream by properly managing the facts that affect it.

Baseline research keeps you focused on your dream by keeping you in control of it—as much as humanly possible anyway. The baseline represents where you are with your dream at this very moment. Once you determine where you are, then you can make better choices about which facts to research and what you need to know about those facts in order to get to where you're going.

Jesus must have established some sort of baseline for his research and realized that his dream, at first glance, appeared to be impossible. There was a law in scripture that had long been enacted: "the law of sin and death."[26] This law exposed the fact that people are imperfect and it identified a time for judging their imperfections—when they cross over into eternity.

On the other side of eternity there is only one place for imperfect people to exist other than within the presence of a perfect God. This alternative is a place not originally created for people: a place of utter darkness and death. Jesus's dream would be possible only if he could investigate the facts and find a way to rescue ordinary people like you and me from such a fate while at the same time satisfying the requirements of the law of sin and death.

The most important facts for you to research are those that most strongly indicate whether or not your own dream is possible. When the facts indicate that your dream is possible, then it is, no matter how farfetched it may appear to be. If your dream were for lightning to strike the same place twice, you might think that could never happen. After all, everyone knows lightning never strikes the same place twice. Yet lightning can be controlled. It can be made to strike where you want as many times as you want.

Positive and negative electrical charges can be measured in the air and on the ground during a storm. If a miniature rocket with a copper wire attached is sent up into the sky at just the right moment, a lightning bolt will appear and follow the wire to wherever it touches the ground. It's an achievable dream because you can learn how to make it happen. More often than not, if your dream seems impossible, it's only because you haven't yet researched the facts in order to learn how to make it happen.

If the facts indicate that your dream is definitely not possible, then you must reevaluate it and adjust some of the details in order to make it achievable. Be careful to avoid completely redesigning your dream because of your research. Facts indicate if and how you might achieve your dream, not what it should be. A dream is strictly an internal discovery originating from your thoughts, emotions, and spirit. It's your destiny because it is created as a result of your legitimate need or personal weakness. A dream cannot originate from facts. Still, you might adjust your dream a little in light of your research in order to ensure that you will be able to achieve it.

Albert Einstein is best known for his theory of relativity. He published more than three hundred scientific works and received the 1921 Nobel Prize in physics. He was named Person of the Century in 1999 by *Time* magazine. Einstein discovered a relationship between science and religion. He said, "Science without religion is lame; religion without science is blind."[27] You discover what your dream is through an introspective search, a type of religious or spiritual experience. Then it becomes worth your while to take a more scientific look into the facts, because they can teach you what to do in order to achieve your dream. Einstein said this willingness to take into consideration both religion and science demonstrates a genuine "aspiration toward truth and understanding" on your part.[28]

On the spiritual side of the equation, consider whether your dream is appropriate or inappropriate in God's eyes. If your dream leads to a questionable lifestyle, then you ought to reevaluate the details of your dream instead of trying to justify your own position. You don't want to take a chance on alienating God since he is the person you will turn to most often for help as you try to take full advantage of the opportunities provided for you by the facts you have researched.

The scientific side of the equation is baseline research. Keep an eye on the big picture. What do you want to accomplish and what do you need to know about the facts in order to accomplish it? Even if you have high aspirations, you can still keep it simple. No need to make the facts more complicated than they have to be. The question is, what facts do you need to learn more about and how can you learn more about them?

Write a description of your dream.

_____

_____

From God's perspective, is your dream appropriate? If not, what aspect of your dream are you going to reevaluate?

_____

_____

What is your baseline? In other words, where are you right now with your dream?

_____

_____

What two or three facts do you need to know about your dream?

_____

_____

What facts are you going to research right away and when are you going to start? What day?

_____

_____

How are you going to conduct your research?

Example: at the library, on the Internet, with classes, periodicals, specialty magazines, how-to videos, seminars, or clubs.

_____

_____

What books are you going to read?

_____

_____

What obstacles might you face along the way?

_____

_____

What do you need in order to conduct your research? How and when are you going to get what you need?

Example: your parent's support, a membership, or money to pay for fees.

_____

_____

You will find it fairly easy to research the facts about your dream and understand all the possibilities as long as you avoid relying solely on your own ideas. Your dream can be achieved only with the help of facts that are well researched. That's the kind of dream God can support. The apostle Paul wrote, "Whatever is true, whatever is noble, whatever is right, whatever is pure, whatever is lovely,

whatever is admirable—if anything is excellent or praiseworthy—
think about such things."[29]

The facts that pertain to your dream are the catalysts that will
enable you to create your dream in a tangible way, in the real world.
They're certainly something you ought to be thinking about. If you
truly understand the facts that apply to your dream, then you can
stay in control. Baseline research helps you do just that.

PART II

Pursuing A Dream

CHAPTER

Now You've Done It!

Now for the exciting part of your dream: pursuing it. You're pursuing a dream that's invisible, so you will need to have faith. An artist creating a sculpture from clay can see the finished sculpture in his or her mind's eye before it has been created. The artist is sure of what he or she is creating and certain that it is just a matter of time before it's revealed. Like an artist you can see your dream taking form and you can practically feel the texture of the clay as you roll your hands gently over it. Nothing is there, of course; you only see it in your mind. The vision you have of your dream is faith at its finest. You're about to bring something entirely new into existence.

The New Testament book of Hebrews provides a list of all the ancient heroes of faith and explains that "faith is being sure of what we hope for and certain of what we do not see. This is what the ancients were commended for."[30] They were commended for the same kind of faith you display as you pursue your dream. Like those ancient heroes, your faith is not a leap in the dark. You are sure about what you're hoping for and certain that your dream is possible even though you haven't seen it happen yet. Now you are ready to join the ranks of those men and women of ancient notoriety.

You are going to transform the abstract into reality and turn an invisible idea into a tangible dream. An achievement like that won't be easy and your faith won't guarantee you a problem-free experience. You'll need to trust God that it will all work out. You are bound to make wrong choices along the way. You cannot get around it. Despite your best effort, it may even appear that your dream is unraveling right in front of your eyes. Even if you feel brokenhearted at times, you must keep trusting that you will achieve your dream. God will mend your heart as you continue to trust that everything will work out.

Some say it's easier to steer a car when it's moving, which means you should get started and work out the details later: take action, get your dream moving, and you will eventually find your way. That's a risky idea because, like an automobile, your dream can break down or run out of gas. A better approach is to establish a sense of trust before you take off. Then that sense of trust will keep you going. It's like buying a map, getting the oil changed, and filling up the gas tank before leaving for your first road trip after getting your driver's license. You're prepared to go mile after mile and get there as soon as possible.

Demonstrate your faith by acting out your dream in a way that's consistent with your friendship with God and also with your assessment of the facts. You are not going to *try* to achieve your dream; you are going to *do* it. Trying means you plan to assess your progress after a while to see if you have gotten any closer. On the contrary, *doing* it means you make your assessment and appeal to

God before you begin. Then you simply trust that your actions will enable you to achieve your dream, demonstrating your faith no matter what the circumstances.

Trusting in his knowledge of the facts, Jesus devised a plan of action to rescue you from your inevitable fate: eternal separation from God. Jesus would be born into the world as a human being at a pivotal point in history, live a perfect life, and never do anything he knew he was not supposed to do. However, in spite of his perfect way of life, in the end he would be subjected to a type of punishment reserved for the worst of wrongdoers.

Jesus would be found by a sophisticated, yet flawed, legal system to be a person who behaved in ways he knew he was not supposed to—exhibiting behavior that was intolerable and deserving of death. Once dead, Jesus would have to be judged again. Then, according to the law of sin and death, he would need to be found to have lived a perfect life as a human being. Only then would it be determined that he didn't deserve the punishment he was given and didn't deserve to be separated from God.

Unlike any other person who came before or after him, Jesus would qualify to live with God in eternity. That being the case, his separation from God would be declared unnecessary and Jesus would be able to offer his separation from God as a payment for someone else. After all, it would be a sacrifice already made; a penalty paid but not owed; a punishment given but not deserved. There would be no sense wasting it. The precedence had already been set through Melchizedek and the Jewish Temple that an eternal high priest could offer a perfect sacrifice. Since he was God and was without sin, Jesus's sacrifice could be offered as a payment in place of not just one other person's separation from God, but as many as would receive it.

Jesus prepared for action by putting his trust not only in God but also in the facts and in his ability to understand and use the facts to his advantage. Yet some think you can change the world simply by trying hard to change it, even if you have to overlook a few facts. You can turn your human will into a harsh taskmaster that can drive you to achieve even the most unreasonable task. Then your fear of failure will push you to do more than you ever thought possible. Therefore, if you're careful to not get bogged down by too many details and you stay focused, you can plow through any obstacle.

The problem with this philosophy is that your dream is not a test of endurance. Pursuing your dream isn't a hard job. You might envision pursuing your dream to be like hacking away at a chunk of coal with a pick axe in a damp, dark mine. However, pursuing your dream is more like tending to a garden. You cannot force your dream to happen. Hard work is going to be necessary, but pursuing your dream through hard work alone is like trying to force a garden to grow. Forget it. It takes a lot of faith to plant and weed your dream and then to trust that over time it will grow into what you want it to be.

Having placed your trust in God and in the facts you have researched to guide your choices, you need only to choose one task to focus on in order to pursue your dream. Then you will finally be pursuing it. With the very first action you take, you will launch off on a journey that could last months or even years. Now is the time to use what you know about the facts to chart your course and ensure that you are starting off in the right direction.

No need to do anything extraordinary to pursue your dream. Just having a dream is extraordinary enough! Keep it simple. Even if you have a big dream you ought to trust that a few simple tasks are enough to get you started. These tasks don't have to be easy, but you don't want them to be too complicated either.

You're ready to review your research and determine what action or series of actions you will take in order to pursue your dream. Your actions are visible affirmations of the faith you have and they demonstrate to the world around you exactly what you're hoping for.

In light of what you still need to know about the facts, what two or three actions are you probably going to have to take, other than research, in order to achieve your dream?

_____

_____

What one action are you willing to take right now in order to begin pursuing your dream? When are you going to start? What day?

_____

_____

What obstacles might you run into along the way?

_____

_____

What do you need in order to be able to take action? How and when are you going to get what you need in order to be able to take action?

Example: a friend's or parent's support, or a specific amount of time or financing.

_____

_____

Rate on a scale of one to ten the degree of certainty you have that you will carry out the action to which you have committed. If your rating is not ten, what prevents it from being a ten? If you have rated yourself less than eight, how can you reduce the action in order to raise the rating to eight or above? If your rating is still below eight, you are unlikely to take action. Go back and review the action that is most important for you to take in order to achieve your dream. Then develop a plan of action you're more likely to complete.

No matter what you do to improve your own situation in life, there are always going to be challenges. When you run into difficulty completing a task associated with your dream it can seem as though it deserves your undivided attention. You may be tempted to make sacrifices in important areas of your life in order to deal with it. When that happens, stop and ask yourself if the sacrifice is really worth it. The area of life in which you're tempted to make a sacrifice may be critical to your happiness and in the end you may find that you didn't need to make the sacrifice after all.

The challenges you will face while completing the tasks associated with your dream will rarely turn out to be as difficult as you might think. To ensure a good outcome you must not spend too much time or energy trying to resolve these challenges. Even the biggest challenge can be easier to deal with when you have a balanced approach to life. Enjoy the important areas of your life that you don't want to put in jeopardy, such as your education, while you're doing whatever you can to work on your dream.

Your dream is supposed to be like a holiday from the normal routine of life. It will make your life more enjoyable, not easier. So plan on working on it occasionally and not obsessing about it. Treat it like a hobby. Do one thing occasionally in order to pursue your dream and be open to what God is doing in your life through it— especially when your other pursuits are causing you stress.

Time shouldn't be an issue. You will do yourself a great injustice if you judge the effectiveness of your actions by the amount of time it is taking you to see results. A dream must take time and be an imperfect process. That way you can deal with the challenges associated with your dream at a comfortable pace and you will have time to personally adapt and grow at the same rate at which you're achieving your dream.

Just as you achieve goals by using your natural talents, learned abilities, gifts, assets, and ambitions, these strengths may also be able to help you with your dream. Take an inventory right now and think about how these strengths might be used to help you achieve your dream.

If you had to identify your best personality trait, natural talent, learned ability, gift, asset, and ambition, what would they be?

_____

_____

If you had to think of one more, what would it be?

_____

_____

Can these strengths help you take action to achieve your dream?

_____

_____

The results of your actions are not measured in terms of success or failure. They're measured in terms of progress. Success is not an accurate measurement of personal achievement. How could it be? Some strange people have found great success. You can think of two or three pop stars, professional athletes, and businesspeople who are very successful, yet downright strange. Their good fortunes appear to be sheer luck more than a measurement of their personal achievements.

Failure is not a sign of a lack of progress either. Some of the most capable people of all time, such as Thomas Edison, were notorious failures. He racked up nearly a thousand failed experiments before developing the incandescent lightbulb that brightens the entire planet. He went through the same process with the phonograph and motion picture camera.

Thomas Edison saw failure as a way to move a project forward. He insisted that "genius is one percent inspiration and ninety-nine percent perspiration."[31] In other words, his inventions were ingenious because he devoted his life to applying what he learned in practical application over and over again—regardless of whether the previous application had failed. Whether you appear to be failing or succeeding, the reality is that you're making progress toward achieving your dream. When you trust the facts to help you make the best choices, you always make progress, no matter how successful or unsuccessful you appear to be.

When it comes to making progress, it's important to focus on doing what you know how to do. Your actions may not bring you immediate results, but the results you desire will come as you keep doing what you know how to do. If your dream is still not turning out the way you want it to and it seems as though fate is working against you, you must not panic! Try to remain enthusiastic. Not about everything—just about the one task you're working on. It's easier to feel enthusiastic if you concentrate your attention on the one task you know for sure will help. What a relief at the end of the day to know that for a little while you escaped from everyday life and worked on one task that definitely got you closer to achieving your dream.

Regardless of your degree of success, your actions should always include prayer, sometimes even prayer with fasting. Jesus is a real person who went through all the ups and downs of pursuing a dream. So he knows what you're going through and he is there to listen and help. Scripture says, "We do not have a high priest who is unable to sympathize with our weaknesses ... Let us then approach the throne of grace with confidence, so that we may receive mercy and find grace to help us in our time of need."[32]

Everyone needs mercy, but not everyone is aware of it. Your dream will place you in a position in which you will be aware that you need God's mercy, and you'll discover that God has "a disposition to forgive," especially when you require compassionate treatment or relief from suffering and God is the only one who can really help.[33] All you need to do is ask.

Pray for grace too. Ask for opportunities that are free gifts from God. After all, your dream is not a self-centered pursuit that you're asking for help with; it's a God-centered pursuit. Your dream is ultimately not about you, but about God and about you having a better friendship with him. God is able to do his best work through the life of a dreamer, and he has designed you to fulfill your destiny for a purpose that only he knows.

Scripture points out that "God chose the weak things of the world to shame the strong ... so that no one may boast."[34] Your dream reflects the need or weakness God has given you so that you might come to realize that you are not self-sufficient. If you take a humble approach to pursuing your dream, God will equip you to be able to turn your need or weakness into an asset or strength.

First you have to do what you know how to do. Then, to a certain extent, you must rest from your work and depend on God—not your own work—to produce the result you desire. It's a humbling experience to identify a need or weakness, define many dreams that will address it, imagine which dream will bring you the most happiness, research the facts about that dream, and then act it out, only to realize that despite your best effort you still cannot expect to achieve your dream without God's help.

The apostle Paul said, "Do not be anxious about anything, but in every situation, by prayer and petition, with thanksgiving, present your requests to God. And the peace of God, which transcends all understanding, will guard your hearts and your minds in Christ Jesus."[35] It's God who has given you your destiny. Spending time speaking with God about your dream enables you to relax and experience real peace. So be quick to express appreciation for the specific ways in which your dream has enhanced your life and for the gracious and merciful ways in which God has granted you assistance. Gratitude is a fantastic emotion to experience and a great friendship-builder. You're drawing closer to the only person who can ensure that the results you desire will come sooner than later.

Turning the invisible thoughts, emotions, and expressions of your spirit into a tangible, visible dream is quite a task. Keep trusting that you are going to succeed and that trust will keep you in the right frame of mind as you work on your dream. Well-placed trust always inspires better choices. Be careful to take action based on the facts, and remember that hard work alone won't be enough, no matter how hardworking, smart, or persevering you are.

You cannot deal with complicated aspects of your dream without God's assistance. Request and accept God's help with humility because in the end it will only be thanks to God that you will ever be able to achieve your dream and finally become the person you really want to be. If you move forward slowly, make the best choices possible, and draw close to God, you can carefully shape your dream into exactly what you want it to be.

CHAPTER

Hope Changes Everything

Andy remembers fishing one morning when he was eight years old. His father was at his side and his fishing rod was propped up with sticks on the lakeshore. It was October and the trees around the lake were glowing orange and red as the sun rose over the horizon. Andy gazed across the lake at several birds playing like children in a schoolyard, but his frustration with fishing overshadowed the entire experience. His rod hadn't moved all morning and eventually he began pleading, "Dad, can we please go home?"

His father replied, "I thought you wanted to go fishing?"

To that Andy declared, "I did, but this is impossible!"

After some convincing Andy agreed to stay just a little longer. But he was sure fishing was something that only adults could possibly enjoy doing. Then the bobber moved and he could hardly believe what he was seeing. It moved again and he yelled out at the top of his lungs, "Dad, Dad, look!" A smile spread across Andy's face as he grabbed his rod. His eyes were wide open and glued to the bobber. He listened to his father's instructions on what to do next. Then he set the hook and reeled in a smallmouth bass.

Later that day as Andy told the story to his mother and friends he insisted, "It was so much fun!" Catching a fish changed from an awkward task to a fun sport once he hoped he might actually catch a fish. A dream works the same way. Like Andy, your perspective will change once you feel a sense of hope. Once you believe your dream might really come true, then you'll be having fun. Andy didn't even have to catch a fish in order to begin having fun. He just needed to see the bobber move.

Hope is the single greatest experience that will motivate you to accomplish your dream. It grabs your attention and keeps you involved by making you feel as though your dream is likely to happen and is worth investing in. Hope is what you experience when your spirit indicates to you from deep inside that the bobber is moving and your dream is achievable and likely to happen. Even in the worst of situations you might suddenly sense, "Wow! Something good is actually going to happen." It's a sense that everything is going to turn out fine. That's when your spirit grabs your attention and stirs you into action.

A strong sense of hope lasts only for a moment, but it leaves an indelible impression. It is powerful, yet fleeting and not to be neglected. If you ignore your emotions they will find a way to torment you until you pay attention to them. Your spirit, however, will grow quiet and shy if you ignore it. You must be sure to take notice when you sense hope—to consciously pause for a moment and relish that sense of hope before it goes away.

Jürgen Moltmann is considered one of the most important German Protestant theologians. He became interested in the subject of hope following his conversion to Christianity in a prisoner-of-war camp during World War II. After his release, Jürgen received his doctorate in theology and became a professor. He experienced a meteoric rise in popularity after writing *Theology of Hope*. In his book *The Experiment Hope*, he explained the difference between "that which *will be* and that which *is coming*."[36] The facts about your dream can indicate what *will be* in the future. Facts prove that your dream *will be* possible. Still, hope is necessary. Hope must be there to encourage and motivate you. Assuming your dream is possible, you really want to know if it *is coming*. Hope tells you that your dream *is coming* and that it might be even better than what the facts have indicated.

The reason you know for sure that your dream *is coming* is that you are already experiencing it in bits and pieces. You are finding clues picked up by your spirit as you experience small achievements resulting from the actions you're taking. These clues cannot clearly indicate what life *will be* like when you finally achieve your dream. Only the facts can tell you that. However, with each achievement and clue your spirit picks up on you realize that your dream *is coming*; you are closer to your destination and further from where you began.

The single greatest sense of hope that Jesus experienced in the pursuit of his dream must have resulted from his resurrection. The circumstances surrounding his resurrection didn't seem very promising at first. He had to search out his disciples three times to further instruct them. Twice he found them "with the doors locked for fear of the Jewish leaders."[37] They were afraid their fellow Jews would turn them over to the Romans as they had Jesus. The third time he found them "going out to fish."[38] That was not how he wanted to keep finding the few men in whom he had invested so much time. He was depending on them to help him achieve his dream.

Regardless of the circumstances the resurrection still gave Jesus a great sense of hope. By raising him from the dead, God had demonstrated that Jesus did not deserve the judgment he was given—that he never did anything he knew he was not supposed to do. So God affirmed Jesus's purity just as Jesus predicted he would.

After the resurrection more than five hundred people met Jesus walking around Jerusalem. Every major Roman and Jewish historian of that time wrote about the event. The resurrection proved that Jesus's life had been completely without sin. It was God's way of demonstrating to the world that Jesus's death had been unnecessary and was therefore a perfect sacrifice. That's just what Jesus had hoped for!

The resurrection opened a way for Jesus to enable people to be with him in eternity. Anyone who wanted to could now face God before dying in order to discuss his or her eternal fate. Jesus knew that for the first time ever anyone on earth could reason with God and say, "I want today to be considered the day I die and see you face-to-face in eternity. I understand that you're perfect and I'm not. I know I cannot exist with you in eternity and there is only one other place for me to exist once I have died. That's a legitimate judgment considering the circumstances. However, Jesus was separated from you even though he did not deserve to be. Will you accept Jesus's death and separation as payment in place of my own separation from you?"

Jesus knew that God could now accept one punishment in place of another, as long as arrangements were made before a person died. At the time of his resurrection Jesus's disciples didn't fully understand that. But the resurrection was still the biggest piece of his dream that Jesus had experienced up to that point. More than ever before he could be sure that his dream *was coming*.

Today you're probably aware that you can ask God to accept Jesus's death and separation as a substitute for your own (see the Preface). When you do that, in God's eyes you die, you're judged, and then you're separated from God. In reality, it's not you; it's Jesus in your place. Afterward you begin a new kind of life in which you won't be required to go through eternal judgment again. Since you're no longer destined to be judged for having done things you knew you were not supposed to do, you are considered to have never done them. Nothing is left to separate you from a perfect God in eternity or in this present life either.

For the first time ever the Spirit of God can now communicate freely and openly with your spirit. It's the equivalent of speaking with God face-to-face in eternity. Only it happens in your spirit here on earth. As with Jesus's resurrection, your new life with God may not appear to be very promising at first because, even though you're going to live with God in eternity, you have to return to your regular life for now. However, despite how circumstances might appear, the Spirit of God "testifies with [your] spirit that [you] are God's children."[39]

According to scripture you begin experiencing heaven on earth when your spirit is made alive or *quickened* with eternal life. It's the same kind of life you will experience in eternity and it's placed within your spirit as a small deposit. So that when you sense this new life, even though you may not be able to put it into words, your spirit knows that heaven is real and that it's coming, because you're already experiencing it in a small way. That's hope!

Scripture says it "is God, who has given us the Spirit as a deposit, guaranteeing what is to come."[40] Our spirit is hopeful that we will indeed experience life with God in heaven as members of God's own family, because we're already communicating with God here on earth, Spirit to spirit. Scripture tells us that "we have this hope as an anchor for the soul, firm and secure."[41]

This is a dream you know you will definitely achieve, even if everything else around you falls away and your hopes and dreams come crashing down. As your heart breaks you can know for certain that not all hope is lost. The most important dream will surely happen for you. You will see God face-to-face and live out your hopes and dreams with those you love in a better place for all eternity. You can always feel confident about that.

Once quickened, your spirit is not only more attentive to the Spirit of God and more aware of the gifts of God, it also begins to more acutely observe and interpret the world around you. That happens primarily through two functions: your intuition and conscience. Your *intuition* draws conclusions without necessarily taking into account all the facts or influences involved. You can feel as though you instantly know exactly what is happening with the same confidence you would have if you had investigated all the facts. Your *conscience* distinguishes between what is right and wrong, good and bad. It is uncanny how your spirit, inspired by the Spirit of God, can so accurately interpret the motives and nature of less-than-obvious people and situations.

Gavin de Becker, author of the best-selling book *The Gift of Fear*, identified the ways in which your intuition might be expressed, including "nagging feelings, persistent thoughts, humor, wonder, anxiety, curiosity, hunches, gut feelings, doubt, hesitation, suspicion, apprehension and fear."[42] Humor, for example, "is a common way to communicate true concern without the risk of feeling silly afterward, and without overtly showing fear."[43] Mr. de Becker told of a company that unknowingly received a package from the Unabomber. As employees debated about what to do with the suspicious-looking package, one of them quipped, "I'm going back to my office before the bomb goes off."[44] Even though he was joking, his intuition was expressing fear. In the end it saved his life.

Your spirit is always at work examining the people and situations around you. Your spirit is perhaps your most personal possession and you trust it emphatically. With it you will unconsciously try to determine whether or not you're likely to achieve your dream. Deep down inside you must know that you have your spirit's endorsement.

Studies show that nearly two-thirds of communication is nonverbal. Your intuition and conscience pick up on this nonverbal communication. Much of what you think people have said to you are words you never actually heard them say. Your spirit is interpreting their actions, looks, and responses. Then you draw conclusions. These conclusions are based on words spoken with gestures and attitudes instead of syllables and vowels.

You communicate more about yourself to people through nonverbal means than by verbal means. Deep down inside you may be struggling with a poor self-image, anger, laziness, or arrogance. You're shocked, however, to discover just how obvious it is to everyone around you. You can try to hide it, but you're only fooling yourself. Nonverbal communication is giving away all of your secrets when you're not looking!

Hope keeps you going when you're wondering, "How did I get here and how am I going to get through it?"—even when it appears that your dream is coming apart at the seams. As an emotion hope is weak; as an expression of your spirit hope is powerful. But the hopeful expressions of your spirit can get mixed up with your emotions. At times it's hard to decipher what's coming from where.

The result is that what you believe to be the expressions of your spirit do not necessarily guarantee what *is coming* in the future. Many Christian leaders throughout history have acknowledged this fact. Among them is the apostle Paul, who said, "I know that good itself does not dwell in me."[45] Having written thirteen of the epistles in the New Testament, Paul knew that his spiritual achievements were the result of a personal struggle, not spiritual infallibility.

Often you must search for a little clarity in order to differentiate between the expressions of your spirit and your emotions. The Spirit of God communicates with your spirit most effectively while you are reading the Bible and praying. These are moments of clarity. When you pray, your spirit is more in tune with what you can expect to happen in the future because you're spending time with "the God of hope."[46] Likewise, when you read the Bible, you find that "everything that was written in the past was written to teach us, so that through the endurance taught in the scriptures and the encouragement they provide we might have hope."[47]

Don't turn to your horoscope for clarity; read the Bible. If it seems too tedious, read another part. It contains law, history, wisdom, poetry, prophesy, four gospels, twenty-one epistles, and apocalyptic literature, which contain messages and lessons that apply to your life. Look for a calendar or Web site that provides daily inspirational Bible verses. If you have a specific question or concern that can be narrowed down to just one word, you can read every reference to that specific word in the Bible using a concordance or Web site such as biblegateway.com. It's a great way to study the Bible.

Jesus assured his disciples of what would happen once he was gone, promising them, "I will ask the Father, and he will give you another advocate to help you and be with you forever—the Spirit of truth."[48] The Spirit of God acts as your counselor. It's always more important to interpret what the Spirit of God is communicating to you through prayer and scripture than it is to try to interpret what is going on with the people and situations related to your dream. The Spirit of God will never leave you to your own devices. Jesus said, "The Advocate, the Holy Spirit, whom the Father will send in my name, will teach you all things."[49]

In 1795, Thomas Paine published *The Age of Reason*, a variety of personal opinions based on his knowledge of the solar system. He argued in favor of a "Creator" and the "inhabitants of worlds [who] behold our earth [from other planets]."[50] However, he called it "conceit" to imagine that God would help people who are "dependent on his protection."[51] Paine believed you *are not* alone—there is a God and even life on other planets. But if you search the Bible in order to find God or go into an empty room to pray, then Paine believed you *are* utterly alone.

Do you ever feel alone, as if no one understands you? Since you aren't capable of fully communicating all of your thoughts and emotions to other people, you will always feel somewhat alone—even in a crowded room. Even though the disciples were sincere in their commitments to Jesus, he told them, "A time is coming … when you … will leave me all alone. Yet I am not alone, for my Father is with me."[52] Likewise, scripture says, "When you pray, go into your room, close the door and pray to your Father."[53] When no one else is around you will realize more than ever before that you *are not* alone. Another person is in the room with you: someone who is listening and truly understands you.

If you wonder whether God is really with you, you cannot know he is there simply because someone tells you he is. You must discover his presence for yourself. You need to find a room, close the door, read the Bible for yourself, and talk with God about what you're honestly thinking and feeling about life. Sometimes you need to calm down, quiet your thoughts and emotions, and meditate on God. In quiet moments God encourages you to "Be still, and know that I am God."[54]

The time you spend alone with God gives birth to hope— the hope that you are not alone; that there really is a God who understands you and loves you deeply—better than you even love or understand yourself! Scripture says, "Hope does not disappoint us, because God has poured out his love into our hearts by the Holy Spirit, whom he has given us."[55]

Thomas Paine tried to prevent you from attempting to communicate with God just as Erich von Däniken is doing today in *Chariots of the Gods*. Both acknowledge the existence of God, but not the God of scripture. Paine wants you to believe the God of scripture is not there while von Däniken wants you to believe extraterrestrials—not God—are responsible for all divine visitations in scripture. Hank Hanegraaff explains that "if extraterrestrials do exist, such a discovery would not nullify Christian doctrine but confirm the extent of God's creative capabilities."[56] Francis Schaeffer was one of the most brilliant philosophers of the twentieth century. He encouraged everyone to communicate with God and to be inquisitive and intellectual, so you can discover for yourself "the God who is there."[57]

The Spirit of God interacts with your spirit in order to help you find God. As you communicate with God you will find hope while you pursue your dream. Hope is a very powerful expression of your spirit. It won't be able to tell you what your life *will be* like once you achieve your dream, but it will assure you that your dream *is coming.*

CHAPTER

Confidence, Compassion, And Conflict

Confidence is more than a desirable personality trait; it is vital to your success. You must possess confidence in order to achieve your dream and become the person you really want to be. Mark Burnett, creator and executive producer of the hit television program *Survivor*, said, "I've heard a hundred times that you can fake confidence, but you can't. It takes too much of a toll. You waste too much energy."[58] If you lack confidence, it is only because it hasn't risen to the surface. Your confidence is hibernating. As the fresh scents of spring draw a bear out of hibernation, your confidence can be coaxed out.

Scripture encourages us to "approach God's throne of grace with confidence, so that we may receive mercy and find grace to help us in our time of need."[59] Confidence to approach God comes from your firm belief that God really hears you when you pray. When Jesus was here on earth pursuing his dream, a close friend named Lazarus passed away. Four days later Jesus cried as he stood in front of the tomb. Then he prayed, "Father, I thank you that you have heard me. I knew that you always hear me."[60] That's what Jesus said just before asking God to raise Lazarus from the dead! Scripture says, "This is the confidence we have in approaching God: that if we ask anything according to his will, he hears us. And if we know that he hears us—whatever we ask—we know that we have what we asked of him."[61] God needs you to be just that confident.

How can you have that kind of confidence while living in such an unpredictable world? It's an especially hard question if you have experienced moments when the stability of your family, your health, or your personal safety have hung by a thread. You may know firsthand how uncertain life can be. Still, confidence can always be drawn out, even in an unpredictable world.

At times you won't have enough confidence to ask God for help and believe he will hear you or help you. When that's the case, you ought to ask God to show you compassion because the more you allow God to leave his own mark on you in the form of compassion, the more your confidence will grow. Compassion is showing "empathy and sympathy for the suffering of others."[62]

After Adam and Eve sinned against God "the eyes of both of them were opened, and they realized they were naked."[63] God could have told them, "I'm done!" Instead "God made garments of skin for Adam and his wife and clothed them."[64] It was the very first act of compassion. It gave Adam and Eve the confidence they needed to face a new way of life, knowing that God was close by and was willing to put himself in their place and sympathize with their sufferings.

Today God shows compassion in a variety of ways. Any occurrence can be considered compassion if it indicates to you that God is close to you, especially when you're suffering. You may experience evidence of God's mercy or grace, or a sensation of hope in your spirit. Or it might just be an idea that comes to mind while you pray or read the Bible, indicating to you that God is indeed your close companion.

The story of Job is among the oldest in the Bible. Job endured a tremendous amount of suffering. Initially, his lack of confidence caused him to employ the same coping mechanisms you may be using today. Job became frustrated, defensive, argumentative, angry, and sad. Yet he eventually realized that the way to cope with the difficulties he faced was to seek compassion from God. It may be difficult for you to recognize that you need compassion too. Like Job, you would rather believe you can handle life on your own with just a little bit of help from God.

Praying for compassion is far more humbling than asking for help, because you must realize and admit that you cannot handle life on your own, even *with* God's help. You need the companionship of God as well. It took time for Job to realize that. He tried to say and do the right things on his own. But he eventually came to the end of himself and found God. Scripture says, "You have heard of Job's perseverance and have seen what the Lord finally brought about. The Lord is full of compassion."[65]

Job tortured himself trying to find all the right answers while also trying to remain confident, even when his wife and friends were not supportive. But it was simply too much for him to handle. Job became convinced that God was trying to hurt him. In the end, however, he learned what a close companion God had been and the extent to which God had actually put himself in Job's place and suffered with him. Perhaps you're not suffering like Job, but you may be struggling, especially if you are passionate about your dream, trying to do your best, and believing you might not succeed. It can seem like torture!

Job's story encourages you to embrace compassion early on instead of trying to cope with your own struggle in other ways. If you're honest with yourself, you might tell God, "I'm afraid I won't succeed. But if you put yourself in my place and struggle with me, perhaps I will come to see what a close companion you really are and that will give me the confidence to go on."

When God leaves his own mark on you in the form of compassion, it builds your confidence in many ways. First it teaches you how to show compassion toward others—to leave the same mark on them that God has left on you. When others (even family members and friends) hurt you or simply irritate you, you will be able to recognize their need for compassion. You will realize that you don't have to figure them out; you just need to show an interest in them as people. And you don't necessarily have to provide answers either. They may simply need you to put yourself in their place, to suffer with them and identify with what they're thinking or feeling. Taking that kind of interest in another person shows real confidence.

Receiving compassion from God also builds your confidence by encouraging you to stand back and observe your own behavior from a more compassionate perspective. You can be way too hard on yourself. But it's possible to objectively place yourself in your own shoes and to show empathy and sympathy for your own suffering. For example, you can try to recognize your favorite coping mechanism and how it prevents you from living a rational life. Seek to understand why it always seems that it will help even though it never does. You can stop paying attention to unflattering memories about yourself. Or you can stop being overly critical of yourself and forgive yourself so you can finally live your life and seek God in peace. Showing compassion toward yourself in these ways demonstrates real confidence.

As Job experienced compassion, it gave him confidence to forgive himself and his friends. He admitted, "I spoke of things I did not understand."[66] Job was willing to "repent in dust and ashes" and confess his faults once he understood that God was compassionate.[67] It feels liberating to confess your faults to a compassionate person—how much more so when you confess your faults to a compassionate God? It feels great! After confessing his own faults, Job prayed for his friends. He put himself in their place and tried to identify with why they had harassed and humiliated him throughout his suffering. Scripture says that "after Job had prayed for his friends, the LORD restored his fortunes and gave him twice as much as he had before."[68]

Scripture points out that "the LORD blessed the latter part of Job's life more than the former part," referring not only to his legendary wealth, but also to a new richness of life.[69] Job experienced compassion through the close companionship of God and it was a glimpse into God's own personality. Speaking metaphorically Job said, "My ears had heard of you but now my eyes have seen you."[70] As God left his mark on Job, it renewed Job's confidence in God and gave him the heart to go on.

Scripture speaks of "being confident of this, that he who began a good work in you will carry it on to completion."[71] This is not self-confidence. It is confidence in God's ability to complete the work he began in you. When Jesus raised Lazarus from the dead, he prayed, "*Father*, I thank *you* … I knew that *you* … I said this for the benefit of the people standing here, that they may believe that *you* …"[72] Jesus's confidence was not self-confidence. He was confident that God was his closest companion and that God would help him achieve his dream and fulfill his destiny, even if it meant raising a man from the dead.

It's possible that you might not achieve your dream—but it's more probable that you will achieve it. At first you may feel a little afraid that you might not be able to do it. However, you will eventually come to accept that you can achieve your dream if God is with you. The following questions will help you receive compassion from God and awaken your own sense of confidence. If you answer no to a question, you should think about why that was your answer.

Are you confident that you can express what you think and how you feel about your dream, and recognize the expressions of your spirit?

_____

_____

Are you confident that you can deal with your need or weakness?

_____

_____

Are you confident that you can research the facts that are pertinent to your dream?

_____

_____

Are you confident that you can take action to begin pursuing your dream right now?

_____

_____

Are you confident that your best personality trait, natural talent, learned ability, gift, asset, or ambition might help in some way?

_____

_____

Are you confident that you will notice when you experience a sense of hope?

_____

_____

Are you confident that you can admit your need for companionship and ask God to put himself in your place and suffer with you?

_____

_____

Are you confident that you will receive compassion from God?

_____

_____

Are you confident that you can show compassion toward others and yourself?

_____

_____

Are you confident that you can finally become the person you really want to be?

_____

_____

Did you answer *no* to any of the previous questions? If so, what exactly are you not confident about? What do you think is likely to happen if you receive compassionate treatment from God, try to do your best, and stick with your dream for an indefinite period of time?

Confidence grows with the knowledge that no matter what the circumstances there is always a chance to identify a need or weakness, define many dreams that will address it, imagine which dream will bring the most happiness, research the facts about that dream, and then pursue the dream as an act of faith. You can feel absolutely confident about that.

A relationship exists between your level of confidence and the value you place on your thoughts and emotions, needs and weaknesses, facts and faith, intuition and conscience, and compassion. It builds your confidence when you place a high value on each of these characteristics because then you know that no matter what you encounter in life the things you value most can never be lost. There is always hope and always a chance to pursue a dream, to get alone with God, and to understand God's personality better.

The confidence that comes with this knowledge is bigger than yourself, bigger than your circumstances and attitude. It gives you the sense that everything is going to work out fine. In fact, once it's brought out into the open, this sense of confidence will often develop into a kind of fearlessness. You may not even be aware when it happens.

Fearlessness will begin to show itself in many positive ways in your life. You just feel as though you no longer need to complain to get your way. You don't have to exaggerate to make a point. You can no longer bear to throw others under the bus in order to get what you want. When you know embarrassing tidbits about others, you keep them to yourself. You stop ignoring facts when you don't agree with them. Others can tell you are not finding fault, placing blame, or acting as phony as you used to. Living your dream fearlessly means you are no longer afraid to be vulnerable, to be straightforward, and to simply be yourself.

Despite its many attributes, fearless confidence is no guarantee of success. Neither is it constant. It is possible to lose confidence occasionally and to give in to wishful thinking or fearful speculation about your dream. Someone once said, "The test of real confidence is that after you lose it, it comes back."[73] That's the nature of a sincere conviction. You grow to believe something so strongly that even if you're distracted for a period of time, you will eventually turn your focus back to it and your confidence will return once again.

You might drift for a while from the confidence you have in what you know to be true about your dream because you want to try an off-the-wall idea just to see what will happen. For a brief moment you may even abandon everything you've learned about pursuing a dream, take the easy way out, and embrace what I call a *could-be frame of mind.*

The could-be frame of mind enables you to live life with no strings attached. After all, it *could be* that your achievements aren't dependent upon anything but yourself. It *could be* that there is no need for facts. You only need to gather a little information about your dream, develop a hypothesis, and tout it as the truth. You figure your hypothesis *could be* true. The future may even prove that you have stumbled upon a brilliant hypothesis. In the end you *could be* right or you *could be* brilliant. Either way, you can get along fine for a while in a could-be world without having to depend upon God or facts. However, there's a catch. You have entered a world in which there is no basis for hope. No real substance and no assistance exist in a could-be world; there's nothing to give you stability and nothing to bolster your confidence.

If you remain in a could-be world long enough, your need or weakness will move back into a predominant position in your life. This change will eventually cause you to return to your dream because you don't want to watch your confidence fade or see the weak, needy version of yourself return. It's embarrassing when others notice that your confidence is fading, especially if this change catches the attention of someone who has given himself or herself completely over to a could-be way of life.

No matter how passionately they seem to express themselves, you can be sure that people who have embraced a could-be frame of mind don't place a very high value on their own thoughts or emotions, needs or weaknesses, or even on facts or actions. Instead they place more value on their appearance, reputation, cash value, ability to work, and ability to learn. They try to keep their focus on the productive activities they're really good at. As far as they're concerned, facts cannot give people confidence because facts don't exist. If facts do exist, they are relative to everyone's own perspective. It *could be* that facts are constantly changing, and it *could be* that there is no correlation between their ability to achieve their own so-called dream and their reliance upon facts.

Fear and defensiveness make sense to those living in a could-be world because the parts of life that matter most to them are extremely fragile and can be lost at any moment: their appearance, reputation, cash value, ability to work, and ability to learn. They're smart to be afraid. In a could-be world fearlessness is simply not possible. They tell themselves that fearlessness is a game played by unreasonable people who really have nothing more than opinions like everyone else. It seems ridiculous to them when Christians with dreams try to prop up their personal opinions by acting as if they're fearlessly confident. Any right-minded person who sees the world from a could-be perspective knows that Christians who act fearlessly confident simply aren't aware of how the real world works. In fact, in a could-be world it even makes sense for them to try to liberate you from the oppressive bondage of a dream that makes you dependent upon facts—especially since your dream also makes you dependent upon God.

As you're not necessarily aware that you are acting fearlessly confident, others don't realize that they are acting as advocates of a could-be way of life. Ironically, this could-be lifestyle enslaves these unsuspecting advocates. Even though it feels liberating, they have become locked into a way of thinking in which they will never have a good reason to be confident. They no longer even suspect that confidence is real or that fearlessness is something anyone could ever truly possess. They simply assume you're putting on an act, just like them. Yet, your freedom is enlarged by a real dream, not diminished. A real dream enables you to accomplish more than you ever thought possible, more than you could possibly accomplish on your own without the facts and God to help you.

Realize that people who have embraced a could-be frame of mind are in conflict with reality. Even though they don't want to believe it, deep down inside they know exactly what is happening—they're destroying themselves. In spite of this experience, they justify their position in their own minds by defending their way of thinking in conversations with others. They will often even commit themselves wholeheartedly to social conflicts in an attempt to hide their own internal conflict—even if it means they have to abandon any adherence to the facts. They're utterly lost in a counterfeit world and cannot believe in real hope any longer. You're capable of falling into despair every once in a while, but not like them. They embrace it and refuse to give it up.

To live in despair is to live the very opposite of hope. A person who is living in despair has convinced himself or herself that ignoring a need or weakness will make it go away. These people define their dreams using their talents, abilities, and strengths. They never find their destiny. Even though they cannot be sure they will ever find happiness, they pursue what they call their dream anyway. Facts aren't necessarily true—God doesn't exist—but they're sure that circumstances can be manipulated. Using their talents, abilities, and strengths, they set off to achieve their so-called dream.

Their efforts aren't as important as their sincerity. As long as they're pursuing their dream with a sincere heart nobody can judge their efforts. However, their efforts are *more* important than the results they achieve. The important thing is that they try, not that they succeed. Success really doesn't matter to them. It's not their fault if they don't achieve their dream. After all, they believe the odds are against them anyway. They believe the way they treat other people has no impact on how far they get with their so-called dream. It is also not a problem if they achieve their dream and don't really become a better person for having achieved it. That was never their wish. They were already the kind of person they wanted to be before they began.

To embrace despair is to search for the wrong rewards, for the wrong reasons, in the wrong ways—to keep getting the wrong results and yet persist anyway to the point of self-destruction. That's the path that people with a could-be frame of mind are on. Even so, they will still behave as if they're unaware of their own self-destructive behavior and continue to justify their own positions by winning social conflicts whenever they can.

You must fight to stay on guard against such conflicts. You may get sucked into a social conflict every once in a while, but you will grow to understand why it's not a good idea to feed the flames. Your dream is one of the best rewards in life. You don't want to put it at risk by fighting meaningless social conflicts. In the end, the real secret to success in any war of ideas is not necessarily winning a conflict. The secret is that the person you're in conflict with might change sides at any moment. You might assume it is not possible for that person to change his or her mind, but it's definitely possible—and sometimes it happens. All you have to do for your part is to live out your dream with confidence.

When others see dreams that are being lived out right in front of them, some will decide they want to pursue a dream too—even if it means changing sides. If you really live out your dream with a confidence that comes from God's compassion toward you and it shows in your compassion toward others, you can leave more influential marks on others than you might think possible. Even if you never get a chance to see others embrace dreams of their own, they have still seen you embrace yours.

It's a bright idea in a dark world, the knowledge that Christians really believe in hopes and dreams. Christians' dreams will forever shine in the darkness of social conflict. They will forever be a light lived out with confidence—a light that can never be dimmed. Over time, many people with a could-be frame of mind will come to understand this light and embrace it.

PART III

Leaving A Mark

CHAPTER

Don't Look Now, But You're In The Lead!

Paradigm shifts occur when you exchange one way of thinking for another. Rudolph Giuliani, former mayor of New York City, watched the entire country experience a paradigm shift in the way it thought about national security. Giuliani helped the residents of New York City through a difficult transition after the September 11th terrorist attacks. He advises everyone in transition to "know what you believe."[74] It applies not only to what you believe about your dream, but also to what you believe about yourself. It's time to stop thinking that you are learning about dreams and start accepting that you're now the expert when it comes to your own unique destiny and dream. This paradigm shift enables you to begin leaving a mark.

Your dream is going to remain in transition until you achieve it. There will be times of uncertainty and suspense, often with no end in sight, unanswered questions, and lots to think about. This is nothing new. Life is filled with transition: new school, new home, new job, new car, new year, new friends, new vacation, new pet, or a new attitude. As with your dream, these are voluntary transitions in which you prepare for a familiar way of life to end and an unfamiliar way of life to begin. Transition isn't always uncomfortable. In fact, you have already begun to comfortably transition into the person you really wanted to be.

You have learned how to value your thoughts and emotions, understand your destiny, identify your dream, pursue happiness, acknowledge facts, act out your dream, cherish hope, embrace compassion, and find confidence in God. You're well equipped to make decisions that will keep your dream moving in the best direction. What other people have educated themselves so well about your unique dream?

Rudolph Giuliani says, "You have to be an optimist. People don't follow pessimists. People follow hope. They follow people who solve problems."[75] In the case of your dream, you must be ready to lead yourself with an optimistic attitude. Being optimistic doesn't mean you have all the right answers or always have a great attitude. It just means you understand that you have acquired knowledge and the wisdom necessary to apply this knowledge. You can feel confident about your ability to make good choices.

Being optimistic means understanding that someone has to accept responsibility for managing your life and you are the nicest and most qualified candidate. You ought to accept responsibility for the job. Of course there are going to be times when you need help from others in order to achieve your dream. You want to be open-minded and willing to ask for advice, but be careful not to put too much stock in the advice you receive. Regardless of how helpful or hurtful other people's advice may turn out to be, in the end *you* are ultimately responsible. Other than God, no one can affect your dream or control your destiny more than you can. You don't want to give up too much of this responsibility to someone else.

Many experts imply that if you listen closely and do exactly what they say, then you can become as much of an expert as they are. Common sense tells you that is not possible. Of course you can learn from their knowledge and experience. But experts cannot experience all there is to know about a topic or communicate all they have learned, just as you cannot comprehend absolutely everything you hear. If it were possible, then before long everyone would be an expert on everything!

Someone will always know a little more than you do about specific topics related to your dream. They may even want to appear to know more than they do. When you ask these people for advice, they often imply that the advice you seek is too complicated for you to understand. But they're probably just doing a poor job of communicating.

If someone asks you to give advice, you ought to give it freely because it's a great way to leave a mark. Dreamers are givers, not takers. Be willing to give your time and attention, to give mercy and forgiveness, and to give others the benefit of the doubt. You know what it means to be weak or in need, so don't take advantage, take the credit, or take control of other people's lives. One of the most effective ways for you to get what you need in order to achieve your dream is to be willing to sacrifice a little to help others get what they need to achieve theirs. That's why a dreamer will often naturally become a leader.

So many people are looking for a better approach to life. You must not underestimate how many people are searching for answers or how capable you are of building friendships with them. You're more than capable of becoming a leader in other people's lives. Go out of your way to discover what others' dreams are. Then as you search for opportunities to achieve your own dream, you can look for opportunities to help them achieve theirs. As opportunities arise or God intervenes, you can advance your dreams together.

Imagine if all of your friends knew what everyone else's dream was—the dream that would enable each one to fulfill his or her own unique destiny. Imagine the fun and camaraderie you would experience—everyone helping to look for opportunities while sharing in one another's successes. Life would be more meaningful and interesting. Don't you think? What a great feeling it is to be able to encourage others to keep pursuing their dreams and, if possible, to help them do it.

You can appreciate the fact that different people are all pursuing their dreams in a similar fashion even though they're trying to accomplish different tasks. With so many different denominational and nondenominational churches, and so many different styles of worship and expressions of the Christian faith, dreams can serve as a unifying factor. As a Christian, you are a member of one family while, at the same time, you are still a unique person. The more unique you are, the better Christianity will function.

Everyone's on a separate journey, yet on the same road. Not a single teenager has a distinct advantage over the rest—not when it comes to dreams. Personal change is challenging for everyone. It's never simple to become the person you really want to be, not even for an expert. Still, you possess a unique mixture of mental, emotional, and spiritual perspectives that enable you to manage your own transition in a way that makes it as easy as possible. You have experienced life in a way that makes you uniquely qualified to make the decisions that will keep your dream moving in the best direction.

H. Jackson Brown Jr. is famous for publishing words of wisdom spoken by others in *Life's Little Instruction Book*, a *New York Times* best seller. Brown reminds you that "an expert in anything was once a beginner."[76] You were a beginner just recently. Now you're an expert—well qualified to make decisions concerning your dream. It wasn't hard. No special skill was required. Now you must choose to accept your own expertise so you can begin to encourage your friends to pursue dreams of their own.

The way to embrace your own expertise is simply to begin making decisions. Experts don't think to themselves, *I'm not sure, so I'm not going to make a decision right now.* Instead they make decisions. Go ahead and make your first decision as an optimistic expert. Decide what nonverbal message you would like to begin sending out to the world around you. In other words, as others watch you achieve your dream and hear you talk about it, what do you want them to perceive about you? How do you want them to interpret what you're saying and doing? What kind of mark would you like to leave?

This decision helps you define what you expect of yourself as an expert. Your decision doesn't dictate what you will feel, think, or do. It simply clarifies the nonverbal message you would like to send, the mark you would like to leave. It is how you expect the world to see you. You don't want your nonverbal message to be "I know my dream sounds silly, but I'll try it for a while just to see what happens." If that's your opinion, then it will come across in what you say and do.

Don't talk yourself out of achieving your dream; talk yourself into it! Your nonverbal message should be something like, "I might be crazy, but I'm crazy with a dream. I'll never know what a dream is like if I never achieve one. So I'm going for it!" Try speaking that aloud in private twice a day for three or four days. What a surprise it is to discover that before long you're in a completely different frame of mind.

It's a real change, not a trick. You are more or less giving yourself permission to be an expert. Try looking in the mirror and telling yourself, "Someone has to manage my dream and you're the perfect person for the job. You have my permission to make decisions about my dream." Even though you don't speak these words to others, they will come across in your conversations as they become a part of your personality. Friends might say, "I think your dream sounds nuts, but you're having lots of fun with it and you seem to think it will happen. I might read *Teenagers Leave a Mark* too." That's a mark you want to leave on others.

It is important to remember not to be afraid to feel a little fear—even as an optimistic expert. You're confronting your most predominant need or weakness head-on. You won't always be able to make your fear go away. Sometimes you will have to feel it in order to face it.

Jesus faced his biggest fear—losing his relationship with his Father while trying to establish friendships with you and me. When he was hanging on the cross about to die, Jesus recognized that he had made it through life without sinning. Yet in the end he had somehow become everything God and people despised, supposedly deserving the worst kind of punishment. As he was receiving this punishment Jesus cried out, "My God, my God, why have you forsaken me?"[77] Jesus must have wondered who would ever follow him after that. Crucifixion was a form of state-sponsored terrorism designed to intimidate people. The message sent to his disciples was clear: if they followed Jesus's example, they would all suffer the same fate.

Despite how he felt at that moment Jesus was closer than ever before to achieving his dream, and he did achieve it. No matter how fearful the experience, God will *not* forsake you. You may not fully understand what is happening or why it's happening to you, but God genuinely needs you to continue facing your fear and pursuing your dream.

Being an expert is a great adventure. It's a process that takes time and is best experienced in a group setting. Contrary to popular opinion, you don't instantly become an expert when you achieve your dream just because you achieved it. It is your journey that makes you an expert, teaching you to take control of your destiny, to embrace your dream, to stop letting circumstances guide your life, to draw closer to God, and to do so together with others.

Scripture explains:

> During the days of Jesus's life on earth, he offered up prayers and petitions with loud cries and tears to the one who could save him from death, and he was heard because of his reverent submission. Although he was a son, he learned obedience from what he suffered and, once made perfect, he became the source of eternal salvation for all.[78]

What an example Jesus set. He went through the same process you have to go through, embracing the adventure and achieving his dream, and doing so along with others. Robert Murray M'Cheyne was pastor and poet at the Church of Scotland from 1835 to 1843. He said, "It is not great talents God blesses so much as great likeness to Jesus."[79] Jesus is the perfect dreamer and the ultimate example for you to follow. He had amazing adventures with God, which he shared with others, and with God's help you can achieve your dream and leave a mark in the same way.

Scripture reminds you that you're a member of "a chosen people, a royal priesthood, a holy nation, God's special possession, that you may declare the praises of him who called you out of darkness into his wonderful light."[80] God has a plan for Christianity and your dream will play a vital role in this plan. Scripture says, "I know the plans I have for you, declares the LORD, plans to prosper you and not to harm you, plans to give you hope and a future."[81]

Everyone must cross a giant gulf that lies between the person they are right now and the person they really want to be. You can take steps with other teenagers in the same direction to cross over to the other side. These steps are clearly explained in *Teenagers Leave a Mark*, like a well-designed bridge. No extraordinary skill is required. Just one step at a time will get you safely to the other side—to your destiny—where you finally get to become the person you really want to be and you get to know God better. Everyone can cross this bridge together and do so at his or her own pace, slow and steady.

Stay on the bridge, stay close to others, and stay close to God. Untold millions of teenagers just like you have never read a book like *Teenagers Leave a Mark*. Many of them will never achieve their dreams or fulfill their destinies because they have no bridge to walk on. Their struggles to achieve their dreams often end with questions never answered, with no one to walk with them, no one to even point them in the right direction. Alone and confused, they pull away from God. They never give up their desire to achieve their dreams, but they never figure out how to do it either. Don't let that happen to you. Stay on the bridge, stay close to others, and stay close to God!

If you run into questions, return to *Teenagers Leave a Mark* for solid answers. The next two chapters contain advice you can use anytime.

Remember that it's best to pursue several dreams at a time. When you're finished reading *Teenagers Leave a Mark*, go back at some point and design a lifelong dream that you can pursue for the long-term, as well as one or more personal dreams that give your life direction and an urgent dream whenever a crisis arises. Having multiple dreams makes life more enjoyable.

Eleanor Roosevelt declared, "The future belongs to those who believe in the beauty of their dreams."[82] If that is true, then the future belongs to you. More Christian teenagers than ever before are actively pursuing their dreams. So are God, Jesus, and the Spirit of God. My hope is that millions of Christian teenagers from all around the world—from every denominational, political, economic, social, and educational background—will pursue the dreams that will enable them to fulfill their destinies. To help make this dream a reality, dreamers like you must become leaders.

Encourage two or three other teenagers to read *Teenagers Leave a Mark* today, or pick up copies for them. Who knows what kind of positive impact you might have in their lives, especially if they are not Christians and might want to know what it means to pursue God as well as dreams of their own.

Take a moment to write down the names of a few friends you want to encourage to read *Teenagers Leave a Mark*. Then later on you can find out what their dreams are and build more dynamic friendships with them.

_____

_____

_____

CHAPTER

Expressing Who You Are At Your Core

The fingerprints on your hands are made up of a dozen different types of lines and patterns, and also tiny sweat glands that are called *eccrine* glands. Your body contains millions of these glands. Nearly half of them are located in your hands, where they secrete sweat to help regulate your body's temperature. As the sweat evaporates a portion is left behind in the ridges of your fingerprints. So when you make contact with other surfaces a residue remains that's an impression of your fingerprints. You leave these marks everywhere you go, on everything you touch.

As with fingerprints, you leave a mark on everyone you meet through your words, actions, and facial expressions. These are impressions of who you are as an individual; however, unlike fingerprints these marks do not always accurately represent what you truly think, how you really feel, or the expressions of your spirit. Still, for better or worse, you leave these marks all day long on everyone you meet.

Let's review three ways you leave a mark on others. Using your hands as illustrations, imagine that the fingers on your right hand represent your *ordinary* pursuits. Starting with your thumb these are your appearance, reputation, cash value, ability to work, and ability to learn. Next, the fingers on your left hand represent your *extraordinary* pursuits. Starting with your thumb these are your destiny, dream, hope, faith/love, and character. Between your right and left hands are your heart and head. These represent who you are at your core—what you think, how you feel, and the expressions of your spirit.

You reach out and leave a mark on others through the pursuits of your hands, *ordinary and extraordinary*, and by expressing who you are at your core. Yet it's who you are at your core alone that defines you. That's also where you find genuine happiness and a richness to life. Scripture says, "There is nothing better for people than to be happy and to do good."[83] This happiness starts at your core and emanates out, enhancing the pursuits of your hands and enabling you to leave exceptionally influential marks on the people around you.

Connecting with God on a personal level is how you find true happiness at your core—talking with God about what's going on in your life and sensing in your spirit where God is leading you. Connecting with God helps you think through issues and decide how you feel. This private conversation is an opportunity to concentrate on an informal exchange of thoughts at your core, where it's safe to be completely vulnerable and authentic.

Regardless of whether you have this conversation at home, outdoors, or at church, you are transported in spirit to a place where you're present with God. Scripture calls this the "Most Holy Place."[84] It's also called the "Inner Sanctuary."[85] Getting there sometimes requires practice. Some people need to be alone to sense that they are truly present with God when they pray; others need to be in a group setting. Some prefer listening to worship music when they pray; others want complete silence. Some stand still when they pray; others pace around the room. Some pray in complete darkness; others like to be outdoors in the sunlight in order to feel God's presence when they pray. If you take your time and figure out how to get in a place where you know you are present with God when you pray, it will definitely change your life.

Scripture says, "Since we have a great priest over the house of God, let us draw near to God."[86] You probably have a pastor or priest you can turn to for help. But Jesus is also your priest. He is always ready to help you enter the Most Holy Place where you can talk with God and find true happiness. All you have to do is ask for his help.

As for the pursuits of your hands, ordinary and extraordinary, Jesus said, "Your heavenly Father knows that you need them. But seek first his kingdom and his righteousness, and all these things will be given to you as well."[87] God's kingdom is experienced at your core. It is described in scripture as "righteousness, peace and joy in the Holy Spirit."[88] Every kingdom is a reflection of its king's personality. The kingdom of God is no exception. God is a righteous, peaceful, and joyful person at his core, regardless of the pursuits of his hands or the ups and downs that are associated with living such a complicated life. When you ask Jesus to help you enter the Most Holy Place and take your time to talk with God, you ought to sense that righteousness, peace, and joy truly are characteristics of God's personality.

Imagine if you could consistently experience righteousness,

peace, and joy throughout the ups and downs of life—to always be in right standing with God, at rest and cheerful at your core. It's possible! Spending time with God in private conversation and reading the Bible for yourself is what causes God's personality to rub off on you. Then the happiness you experience at your core will improve the marks you leave on others, even the marks you leave through the pursuits of your hands. That is how the kingdom of God is meant to work.

Life is an amazing gift, but some people have a hard time treasuring it. In the United States where the standard of living is among the highest in the world, the homicide rate is also "among the highest in the industrialized world."[89] Even more shocking is the fact that there are twice as many suicides as homicides committed every year. These are people who may have tried to treasure life, yet in the end didn't believe it was possible. As with life itself, true happiness is a gift to be treasured. But you may find it hard to do.

When you're feeling unhappy, you tell yourself it is someone else's fault and then you try to take away their happiness (happiness homicide). If not, you tell yourself your unhappiness is your own fault and react by sabotaging what little happiness you do have (happiness suicide). You're convinced that it's not possible for you to be truly happy anyway—not in certain areas of life.

You continue leaving a mark through the pursuits of your hands and by expressing who you are at your core. But the marks you leave represent your own personality without God's influence. Flawed aspects of your personality show in the marks you leave. Instead of helping others to be happy, you continually antagonize them and enflame the flawed parts of their personalities. You can end this cycle by spending time with God in private conversation and reading the Bible for yourself. The more that God's personality rubs off on you, the happier you will be and the better the marks will be that you leave on others. The choice is yours.

You might avoid spending time with God because the conversation is not all about you and you're not in control. Yet life is never all about you—that's reality. When people commit murder or even suicide, it's an unconscious attempt to take control of life for whatever reason. Likewise, you unconsciously try to control your own happiness either by destroying the happiness of others or by sabotaging your own. The only way to find and maintain true happiness is to see it and appreciate it as a part of God's personality and then simply treasure it in your own life and try not to control it.

Scripture says, "The LORD, whose name is Jealous, is a jealous God."[90] God is jealous that you give so much time and attention to yourself and to so many other people. He enjoys spending time with you and hopes that you will want to spend time with him simply because you like him. It's easier to pay attention to others because you can control the conversation. That is not the case when you spend time with God. You're obliged to be honest with him because he knows you better than you know yourself. That can make you feel vulnerable and uncomfortable. You want to have a discussion in which you influence God, but instead you're there for God to influence you. If you're trying to make the right impression on God while he is trying to leave a mark on you, you're going to have difficulty spending time with him.

God wants to leave his own tangible mark on you so that his personality can visibly affect you. If you want the same, you cannot fake it. You must spend quality time together with God in order for visible effects to genuinely appear. No matter what thoughts occupy your mind, you should discuss them daily with God in great detail. He really is a happy person who is right with the world, at rest, and cheerful at his core. That's the kind of person you want to spend time with. If you become more like him, people will want to spend more time with you too!

It's comforting to find true happiness at your core while you're waiting to achieve your dream. It's natural to be excited about what you want. Yet you cannot always have it right away. The anticipation is enough to drive you bonkers. Your dream is supposed to be challenging, and you must be prepared to ride it out. There will be ups and downs. The downs are the problem—the times when it seems as though it's taking forever.

Some things in life matter to you far more than they should: good and bad things, helpful and hurtful things. When your dream matters too much, when you want more than you are able to have, you set yourself up to become the person you don't want to be, in hot pursuit of something you cannot have right away. That can lead to despair, anger, resentment, and sadness at your core. This frustration filters through to the pursuits of your hands and shows in the marks you leave on others. Then the people you care about the most are bound to suffer as you try to force your dream to happen faster than it possibly can.

You might go off anyway, declaring war on the world around you, embarrassing yourself and steamrolling over people you ought to care about. You believe there has to be something you can do or someone you can confront in order to get your dream to move along faster. In the end, however, you will discover that no one wins in these situations. Little wars never help matters and your attitude only isolates you.

Booker T. Washington was freed from slavery following the Civil War. As a young man he experienced what it meant to deal with personal challenges. Economic conditions forced him to accept work as a salt-packer, coal miner, steamboat hand, and houseboy. However, Washington's hard work paid off when he was given the opportunity to learn how to read and write.

Washington loved learning and eventually obtained a formal education. Afterward he dedicated his life to helping others. As an educator, author, and African American civil rights leader, he represented the last generation of black leaders who had been born into slavery. Washington was the most powerful African American in the nation from 1895 to 1915. He explained that "there are two ways of exerting one's strength: one is pushing down, the other is pulling up."[91]

When you feel frustrated, you ought to communicate in positive ways with those you care about instead of driving them away. Pull them up instead of pushing them down. Take advantage of friendships instead of neglecting them. Take an interest in learning something new about others. Ask for advice. You might actually learn something new—even from those you wanted to go to war with. You just might discover that you're not the first one to experience this sense of frustration. What usually happens is that you hear stories that are surprisingly similar to your own. The way you feel the world is treating you is not uncommon and it's nothing personal. You are not the first one to go through it and you are certainly not going to be the last.

It is amazing how much better you can feel after discovering that everyone is in the same boat. This sense of camaraderie helps you see that it's not the end of the world if you cannot have what you want right away. Knowing that everyone else has to wait for his or her dream can make you feel more content. You can focus on who you are at your core and relax the grip you have on the pursuits of your hands, knowing that nothing will be lost.

It's easy to think your friendships will take care of themselves. Extra time may seem better spent catching up on your dream instead of spending time with those you care about. Still, your friendships ought to take priority over your dream. It's a great way to leave a mark on others—simply expressing by the way you live your life that who you are at your core is more important than the pursuits of your hands and your friendships are more important than your dream. It's amazing how much better you can feel and how much more productive you can be after making who you are at your core and your friendships your first priorities.

Love is a desire not only to make your friendships and who you are at your core your first priorities, it's the desire to constantly improve on them. Don't just wait for others, but be patient. Don't just help, but be kind. Don't just give, but trust. Love is a personal commitment to try not to be envious, behave rudely, become angry, or enjoy the misfortunes that others run into. Malcolm Forbes, publisher of *Forbes* magazine, said, "Keeping score of old scores and scars, getting even and one-upping, always makes you less than you are."[92] Love means restraining yourself from bragging, being proud, and investing only in what is best for you. It means persevering instead of striking back at others—even when they panic, isolate themselves, and declare war on you.

These characteristics of love are easier to express at your core when you have first been able to recognize them as characteristics of God's personality. Again, these are tangible marks God leaves on you. Scripture says, "Love comes from God. Everyone who loves has been born of God and knows God."[93] You can act nice toward others. But when you need God's love in so many different ways and you sense that you have his love, you can find within yourself the ability to express the same love in your friendships with others—even in your friendship with God.

God wants to be loved. That may seem odd. It's easy to never think about how you act toward God, to never consider whether you are being patient and kind, or acting rude and angry toward him. You might figure God has big shoulders and can handle it. After all, you have to constantly wrestle with God anyway. You beg for help, wait and wait, and beg some more. God hears your prayers and wants to answer you. Like anyone else, though, God also wants to be loved.

When Adam and Eve were in the Garden of Eden, God enjoyed spending time with them "walking in the garden in the cool of the day."[94] God hoped they would treasure their friendships with him more than their pursuits of knowledge, but that was not the case. It must have hurt God's feelings. Today you are challenged to value your own friendship with God more than the pursuits of your hands. Then you will be able to recognize the characteristics of love in God and mimic them in your friendships with others, as well as in your friendship with God. You have this encouragement from scripture that "love never fails."[95]

In addition to being an expression of your thoughts and emotions, love is also an expression of your spirit. When your body dies, your spirit will continue to live on in a way that is somewhat similar to your mortal life here on earth. Scripture says that after death, "these three remain: faith, hope and love."[96] These are "theological virtues" that exist right now within your spirit.[97] According to C. S. Lewis, "As a rule, only Christians know about [them]."[98] Lewis was an intellectual of the twentieth century who wrote *The Screwtape Letters*, *The Chronicles of Narnia*, and *Mere Christianity*.

The theological virtues of faith, hope, and love go hand-in-hand with pursuing a dream. The Spirit of God helps you develop them in your spirit as you get to know God better. They show in the marks you leave on others as you express who you are at your core. They're assets that you take with you in your spirit when you cross over into eternity. The effort you put into developing them right now is always worthwhile and never in vain because you will pick up where you left off when you get to heaven.

Hank Hanegraaff is one of the world's leading Christian apologists, a best-selling author, and host of the *Bible Answer Man* radio program. Hank points out that "heaven will be a place of continuous learning, growth, and development. By nature, humans are finite, and that's how it will always be. While we will have an incredible capacity to learn, we will never come to the end of learning."[99]

In heaven, God will still be all-knowing and we won't be. God is a unique person who is omniscient (all-knowing), omnipresent (present everywhere at the same time), omnipotent (all-powerful), and so complex that even in eternity you will never be able to know or understand God completely. You too are unique, complex, and difficult to understand, and your life will become even more complicated when immortality gets added into the mix. It means that in heaven you will forever be challenged to grow and develop personally.

You cannot imagine the adventures you will have pursuing your dreams in heaven. Sometimes it can seem as if your mortal life here on earth is full of excitement and heaven may turn out to be dull and disappointing. Just the opposite is true. In heaven you will forever be learning, growing, developing as a person, and enjoying countless friendships.

Faith, hope, and love are virtues you will continue to develop for all of eternity, but scripture says, "The greatest of these is love."[100] Everyone needs a dream. You need love too, and you cannot enjoy pursuing your dream without it. Love makes you happy. When you express love, you're reflecting the characteristics of God that are at your core, being more the person you really want to be, having positive effects on others, and generally making the world a better place. Here are some questions that can help you better express love.

Who loves you? Not who is *supposed* to love you. Who in your life is actually patient, kind, and trusting of you in a variety of situations?

Example: a grandparent, friend, religious leader, parent, and/or God.

_____

_____

What are some appropriate ways to show them that you appreciate their love?

Example: Thank them for their support. Write a thank-you letter or send them an e-mail to say you were thinking about them. Grab your phone and send a text, or call them and say "thanks!"

_____

_____

Do you treat God in a loving way? Are you often patient with, kind to, and trusting of God? What one aspect of love would you like to express more often toward God?

_____

_____

Do you treat yourself in a loving way? Are you often patient with, kind to, and trusting of yourself? What one aspect of love would you like to express more often toward yourself?

_____

_____

What friendships are most important to you? Who do you most want to treat in a loving way? Who do you hope feels genuinely loved by you?

_____

_____

What is one simple way you can express more love for each person who you mentioned above? Brainstorm and think of some fun ideas.

Example: Ask them out to lunch or a movie—anything to create more interaction with them. If you want to express more love toward God, then help those who are less fortunate; in doing so you have helped God.

_____

_____

Is there anyone you know right now who seems to be drawing back and declaring war on those around him or her? How can you show this person mercy in his or her distress and look beyond any irrational behavior and show empathy?

_____

_____

Is there anything you would like to do to show a perfect stranger that someone cares about him or her?

Example: Donate time or money to a homeless shelter or third-world orphanage once or twice a year. Or you can simply say hello to someone who looks lonely.

_____

_____

It's fun to answer the same questions at the end of the day in the form of a journal so you can gain a sense of accomplishment. Below are sample journal questions. The challenge is to answer them at the end of the day, several days a week for just a couple of weeks. You will discover how loving you can be. Try it and see if someone makes a comment about your attitude. More important, see if you like the more loving person you're becoming and how it shows in the marks you leave on the people around you.

Who expressed a loving attitude toward you today? How did you show them in an appropriate way that you appreciated it?

_____

_____

How did you foster a friendship or relationship today?

_____

_____

Did you love God today? Were you patient with, kind to, and trusting of God?

_____

_____

Did you love yourself today? Were you patient with, kind to, and trusting of yourself?

_____

_____

What friendships were most important to you today? Who did you go out of your way to treat in a loving way today?

_____

_____

Did anyone seem to be drawing back and declaring war on others? How did you show that person mercy in his or her distress? How could you do it tomorrow?

_____

_____

Did you do anything today to show a stranger that someone cares about him or her?

_____

_____

You ought to have fun leaving a mark on others and expressing who you are at your core. For some people it's a basic necessity: food, water, shelter, and fun. If you're a self-conscious or stoic person, you still need to have fun expressing yourself. If you lose your sense of humor, you might lose your ability to properly leave a mark.

Thomas Aquinas was a Dominican friar from the thirteenth century who was an extremely productive person. He lived in a state of voluntary poverty and chastity, spending nearly all of his time studying, lecturing, and debating. During his short life, Thomas wrote sixty books covering nearly every subject and was "unquestionably the most systematic political philosopher of the Middle Ages."[101] He was a scholastic superstar of his time, serious and single-minded. Yet Thomas also believed in having fun. He took time out of his busy schedule to write about amusement.

Thomas insisted that having fun "is useful for human living. As man sometimes needs to give his body rest from labors, so also he sometimes needs to rest his soul from mental strain that ensues from his application to serious affairs. This is done by amusement."[102] Here is a man who wrote ten million insightful words during a lifetime of only four hundred and thirty-eight thousand hours, sometimes dictating to three scribes at once about different topics. If *he* found time for amusement, you can too.

Amusing activities help you forget about your cares for a moment. They distract you to the extent that you stop thinking about anything important, even the pursuits of your hands and who you are at your core. That's what amusing activities are supposed to do—give you a moment of rest. Having fun for even a brief moment can feel like a breath of fresh air.

Scripture says, "When God gives someone wealth and possessions, and the ability to enjoy them, to accept their lot and be happy in their toil—this is a gift of God. They seldom reflect on the days of their life, because God keeps them occupied with gladness of heart."[103] God wants you to be content and have fun in life. In fact, you ought to be proactive about having fun, finding ways to amuse yourself whenever possible. Just be careful to do so in ways that aren't harmful.

The Spirit of God will remind you that when amusing activities are over, some leave you feeling worse than when you started while others leave you feeling relaxed. Some tempt you to neglect the pursuits of your hands while others motivate you to return to them. Some leave you empty at your core while others energize you to believe in even greater levels of happiness. Instead of participating in sinful activities for fun, you ought to consider allowing the Spirit of God to direct you to morally neutral activities that are just as amusing and far more satisfying. You can trust the Spirit of God to guide you, even when it comes to having fun. Scripture says, "The mind governed by the Spirit is life and peace."[104]

It will be an enjoyable experience when you finally achieve your dream. But achieving your dream won't change you into a happy person. The person who is happiest after achieving their dream is the one who was already happy before he or she achieved it. You cannot stress and strain trying to pursue your dream and then expect to suddenly begin having fun just because you achieved it. Choose to begin having fun right now while you're leaving a mark on others and expressing who you are at your core. Then you will have all kinds of fun when your dream finally happens.

Life is short—too short to go around not having fun. You may only have twenty to thirty thousand days to live. Your attitude ought to be, "Today is my 6,145th day and nothing is going to ruin it for me. I'm going to have fun today, express who I am at my core, leave a mark, and be the person I really want to be."

Having fun may take practice. For an entire day, try to smile about everything that happens to you, no matter what happens. It's easier than you might think. See how much more fun your life can be and how much easier it is to smile the next day.

You have to be able to smile, to think about what is fun about your experiences and to laugh about them. You may feel that you're obligated to be sad or that it's in your best interest to get mad if circumstances don't go your way. But it simply isn't true. You can often still smile and have fun if you really want to. Try writing down two or three humorous thoughts right now that relate to expressing who you are at your core and leaving a mark on the people around you—thoughts you can force yourself to laugh about or at least smile at.

What is fun or humorous about you trying to achieve your dream?

_____

_____

What is fun or humorous about what others think about your dream?

_____

_____

What is fun or humorous about you becoming a more loving person?

_____

_____

What do you think will happen if you try to smile for an entire day about everything that happens to you?

_____

_____

You have gained a balanced approach to life by learning how to leave a mark through the pursuits of your hands, *ordinary and extraordinary*, while not forgetting that it's who you are at your core that matters most. Life is all about expressing who you are at your core and embracing your interactions with others. You will be more comfortable leaving a mark when you begin by finding happiness at your core—a happiness and richness to life that comes from God.

As you spend time with God in private conversation and read the Bible for yourself, you will realize that God really is a happy person who is right with the world, at rest, and cheerful at his core. As God's personality rubs off on you, you will recognize this same sense of happiness at your own core. Then you will be energized to express yourself in more meaningful ways—especially in faith, hope, love for others, and love for God.

Make sure that expressing who you are at your core and leaving a mark is fun. Your first response to challenging or surprising situations may be to become angry or frustrated and not to recognize what is fun or humorous about your circumstances, but practice will change that.

CHAPTER

God's Amazing Master Plan

In order to understand God's amazing master plan you must first know more about his dream. You're a dynamic part of God's creation and a critical part of his dream. As you get closer to achieving your dream and fulfilling your destiny, you will gain insightful glimpses into God's dream. You will find that you can actually help God achieve his dream and share an amazing adventure with him. He has devised a master plan that makes it possible.

God created the idea of *destiny* by demonstrating it for you, not by making it a decree. Perfection is the only weakness, of sorts, that God will ever experience. It's not truly a weakness, but definitely a challenge. Long before the human race was created, perfection posed a question God had to answer. That is, how would he express his own perfection, in tyranny or benevolence? God's answer to this question enabled him to transform what may have seemed like a weakness into a strength and it demonstrated for the first time ever the idea of *destiny*.

Tyranny is the "unrestrained exercise of power," and it was a realistic option for God.[105] It would have been justified in God's case. If anyone should have been placed in a position to exercise power over everyone else, it ought to have been God, since he is perfect. Perhaps it would have been the most humane course of action for God to have taken in the very beginning. He certainly would have made all the best choices for everyone.

Since he is perfect, God must have perceived that despite how perfect he was and the good he could do, it would have been self-serving for him to exercise unrestrained power over everyone else. So it would have been wrong, even though he knew we would all make poor choices when left to our own devices. Instead of trying to make those choices for us, God was committed to giving us the freedom to choose for ourselves. He was also committed to giving us the help we would need to make the best choices possible. God chose benevolence: "an act of kindness; a charitable gift."[106] He chose to give. It was a more complicated way for God to express himself and it turned his perfection into a strength.

When he identified his destiny (to turn perfection into a strength) and designed his dream (to give), God himself established a pattern for everyone else to follow. In that moment it instantly became the godly way to live. Now you can challenge yourself to follow God's example and embrace your own destiny.

God could have chosen differently. How good it would have felt for God to have accepted his own perfection so he could indulge himself in it. No one could have stopped him or even looked down on him for doing so. Even now he could still change his mind and decide to force us to recognize his perfection and to be subservient to him. It's what you would do if you were perfect and you were God. You're not as likely as God to challenge yourself. Instead you're more prone to accept an obvious need or weakness as being a natural part of yourself, especially if it feels good when you indulge in it. But God continues to challenge himself to be benevolent.

You have received so much from God, including his very image. Even though you're the primary recipient of God's benevolence, you're not God's dream. God is a unique person with his own dream, which is to give. By making an effort to receive from God you can help him achieve his dream and fulfill his destiny.

Receiving from God means being open to the mystery of his amazing master plan. When Jesus had done everything possible to achieve his dream, his disciples asked him, "Lord, are you at this time going to restore the kingdom to Israel?"[107] Jesus was ready but he chose instead to remain open to God's plan. So he told them:

> It is not for you to know the times or dates the Father has set by his own authority. But you will receive power when the Holy Spirit comes on you; and you will be my witnesses in Jerusalem, and in all Judea and Samaria, and to the ends of the earth.[108]

Jesus didn't command his disciples to be his witnesses. Instead he said, "You will *receive*," and, "You will *be*."[109] He referred them to God's plan—an amazing plan in which they would experience for themselves God's benevolence and his giving personality.

When the day of Pentecost arrived it became clear to Jesus's disciples that they were participating in the birth of the church. What an adventure that must have been! As a direct result of the disciples' willingness to remain open to God's plan, an estimated one billion people have converted to Christianity throughout two millennia. Another two billion Christians are estimated to be living today.

Much of God's master plan is yet to be revealed. In addition to his commitment to be with you forever, the two greatest gifts God has given you are his Son and Spirit. Receiving God's Son and Spirit into your life is an integral part of being open to God's plan today. *Teenagers Leave a Mark* has presented an explanation of Jesus's destiny and dream, and how to experience more of Jesus's presence in your life. It's easy to experience more of the Spirit of God's involvement in your life too.

The Spirit of God wants to help you. You see this desire to help expressed in many ways throughout scripture. When "God created the heavens and the earth ... darkness was over the surface of the deep, and the *Spirit of God* was hovering over the waters."[110] When Jesus was ready to enter the world as a human baby the angel Gabriel told his mother, "The *Holy Spirit* will come on you, and the power of the Most High will overshadow you."[111] When he was ready to begin his earthly ministry, "Jesus was baptized ... and the *Holy Spirit* descended on him in bodily form like a dove."[112] When the church was birthed, "a sound like the blowing of a violent wind came from heaven and ... all of them were filled with the *Holy Spirit*."[113] When the good news about Jesus was shared with non-Jewish believers for the first time, "while Peter was still speaking ... the *Holy Spirit* came on all who heard the message."[114] Whenever God has taken action in a significant way the Spirit of God has been there to help.

The Spirit of God's *destiny* is to help. It's a heartfelt desire that will never go away. Today, the Spirit of God helps you to have a meaningful friendship with God, for your own quality of life and for the growth of the church. God wants to have a close friendship with you. In order to help, the Spirit of God engages you, Spirit to spirit. The Spirit of God's *dream* is to engage you. When you allow the Spirit of God to do so, you become more attentive to God's amazing master plan, you receive from God more easily, and you're able to get to know God better as a person. So the Spirit of God's destiny is *to help,* and the Spirit of God's dream is to *engage you* one-on-one.

Jesus said, "Flesh gives birth to flesh, but the Spirit gives birth to spirit."[115] He explained that when you become a Christian and receive eternal life into your spirit, this new life enables you to communicate with God, Spirit to spirit. It's as if you start life over. You are "born again."[116] Your spirit was there all along, but it was not alive the way it was designed to be. You were not experiencing life the way you were meant to experience it.

All that changed once your spirit became alive and started to function properly. During natural childbirth there are many changes. Your umbilical cord is cut and a hole in your heart closes. Your lungs oxygenate, your kidneys filter, and your GI tract starts absorbing nutrients. All of this change is just the beginning of prolonged periods of infancy, childhood, and adolescence. It's similar with you spiritually. Spiritual birth is a beautiful expression of life that brings with it changes and growth.

You cannot overestimate the passion with which the Spirit of God engages you to help you grow throughout your spiritual infancy, childhood, and adolescence. At first you might assume the Spirit of God will simply change you into the person you really want to be. Jesus's disciples assumed he would change their lives by changing the world they lived in. Instead he challenged them to change as individuals by saying, "Unless you change and become like little children, you will never enter the kingdom of heaven."[117]

The Spirit of God doesn't change you either. Instead the Spirit of God challenges you to change as an individual and then gives you what you need to be able to do it. Just as the disciples did at Pentecost, you *receive* so you will *be*. You *receive* from the Spirit of God so you will *be* able to grow spiritually, *be* open to God's plan, and *be* prepared for an amazing adventure!

One of the few aspects about you that will instantly change is your body when you die. Scripture says, "You will roll [your body] up like a robe; like a garment [it] will be changed. But you remain the same."[118] The disciples interacted so closely with Jesus that it was natural for them to think he would simply change everything. Likewise as you are engaged by the Spirit of God it's easy to think you will somehow be instantly changed on the inside. But the Spirit of God wants to help you grow, not make you change.

The Spirit of God will help you grow in your gifts and goals, destiny and dream, thoughts and emotions, and in your spirit, all while challenging you to see that there is still something more. It's "the plan of him who works out everything in conformity with the purpose of his will."[119] It is intriguing to discover that beyond who you are and how you apply yourself, there is still something more— an amazing master plan that supersedes even God's own dream, Jesus's dream, and the Spirit of God's dream.

All of these dreams, including your own, are a part of the same master plan that is so much bigger than everyone's dreams. Much of this plan is beyond your understanding and all of it is beyond your control. Yet the Spirit of God is still committed to helping you play a role in it, which requires growth. When Jesus chose his disciples he looked for people who were weak when it came to politics, economics, and even religion. Then the Spirit of God helped them grow. Empowered by the Spirit of God they literally changed the course of human history—all according to God's master plan.

God's plan is still the same today. Scripture explains that God's intent is that "through the church, the manifold wisdom of God should be made known to the rulers and authorities in the heavenly realms."[120] Scripture also says, "Christ loved the church and gave himself up for her to make her holy ... to present her to himself as a radiant church, without stain or wrinkle or any other blemish."[121] When you see the church in its current condition, sometimes it is hard to imagine that it could represent the wisdom of God in the world. It is equally hard to imagine that the church could ever be without blemish—but that is God's plan!

For centuries, humanity has benefited from teenagers just like you who were open to playing a role in God's plan. Humanity is God's primary concern. He is concerned about other issues as well, such as the environment, but humanity is his primary concern. Humanity is unique in the universe and highly valued because every individual is a living being with a soul, made in the image of God. The world and everything in it is passing away, including your own body and your physical ties to this world. But you have an opportunity in God's amazing master plan to focus less on the desires and disappointments of this world and to play a role in something that will leave a permanent mark on other human beings.

The Spirit of God values you above everything else in this world. More than ever before the Spirit of God is attempting to engage you in order to grow within you what scripture calls the "fruit of the Spirit."[122] It's one fruit with nine attributes—love, joy, peace, patience, kindness, goodness, faithfulness, gentleness, and self-control. These are characteristics of God's personality that are masterfully grown over time by the Spirit of God in your own spirit and personality.

Do you recognize these attributes as characteristics of God's personality? If not, then tell God "I hope you love me, feel joy and peace when you think about me, and are patient with me in the future. I want to know you're kind, good, and faithful. Be gentle and self-controlled when you're helping me." How much better would life be if you knew these attributes were characteristics of God's personality and knew you could experience more of them in your own spirit and personality? That's part of God's master plan.

Only a benevolent God with a perfect personality and amazing plan can change the world and grow the church by producing the fruit of the Spirit in the lives of so many different kinds of people. This plan was conceived and put into practice at the beginning of time with the Spirit of God's help.

The world tells you in a variety of ways that by taking a scientifically pragmatic approach to life you can develop a high quality of life on your own, and positive character traits such as the fruit of the Spirit, without God's help. But science cannot help you with the most personal aspects of your life. Electronics are produced by a perfect kind of science, but many fields of science are not so perfect. The scientists in these other fields of study often give out information that is either not entirely factual or completely misleading—sometimes out of speculation and other times because of competition. For example, the theory of evolution has given birth to scientific research that has been manipulated and then misrepresented as scientific fact.

New light has been shed on many claims regarding fossil records. Scientists and professors claimed that both *Archaeopteryx* and Pro-Avis were the missing links between reptiles and birds. It was later revealed that "*Archaeopteryx* is a full-fledged bird, not a missing link."[123] It was also discovered that "no fossil evidence exists for Pro-Avis."[124] Then there was "Punctuated Equilibrium," which was a recreation of "Goldschmidt's hopeful monster theory"—further investigation proved both to be insufficient explanations for the missing link.[125]

For many decades teachers and professors have touted Nebraska man, Java man, Piltdown man, and Peking man as the missing links between primates and humans, using textbooks laced with erroneous scientific claims. The fact is "a single solitary tooth of a wild pig [was used to build] Nebraska man and Nebraska woman, *Hesperopithecus haroldcookii*."[126] "*Pithecanthropus erectus*, called *Homo erectus*, nicknamed Java man, [was built with only] a skullcap, femur [and] three teeth. The femur was found fifty feet from the skullcap a year later."[127] They couldn't possibly go together. "Two human skulls [were also] found in close proximity."[128] "Piltdown man, *Eoanthropus dawsoni*, [was] the jaw of an ape stained to make it appear as though it matched a human skull. Not only stained but also reshaped."[129] "It was formally declared a fake."[130] "Peking man [came from] fourteen [crushed] skulls and an interesting collection of tools and teeth."[131] "The skulls found were merely those of monkeys."[132]

Scientists and professors have also employed flawed scientific experiments to prove chemistry's supposed role in the theory of evolution. Walter L. Bradley, PhD is author of *The Mystery of Life's Origin*. He has explained in great detail why a landmark experiment in 1953 by Stanley Miller and Harold Uery was an elaborate hoax that has been touted for decades as the final answer to the question of how life originally sprang from a simple chemical reaction. Miller and Uery were "smart enough to know that if you start with inert gases like nitrogen and carbon dioxide, they won't react."[133] So

Miller used different chemicals even though there wasn't "any real proof that the earth's early atmosphere was composed of ammonia, methane, and hydrogen, which Miller used in his experiment."[134]

In reality, says Bradley, "From 1980 on, NASA scientists have shown that the primitive earth never had any methane, ammonia, or hydrogen to amount to anything. It was composed of water, carbon dioxide, and nitrogen—and you absolutely cannot get the same experimental results with that mixture."[135]

Lee Strobel took Miller's flawed findings one step further and discovered that "even if Miller had been right about the ease with which amino acids could be produced in the primitive earth's atmosphere, nevertheless the process of putting them together into protein molecules and then assembling those into a functioning cell would be mindboggling."[136]

According to Bradley, "Amino acids come in eighty different types, but only twenty are found in living organisms. The trick is to isolate only the correct amino acids [which] have to be linked together in the right sequence to produce protein molecules." It sounds simple enough, but there are other complicating factors.

> Other molecules tend to react more readily with amino acids than the amino acids react with each other [and] amino acids are right- and left-handed, and only left-handed ones work in living matter. Now you've got to get only these select ones to link together in the right sequence. And you also need the correct kind of chemical bonds—namely, peptide bonds—in the correct places for the protein to be able to fold in a specific three-dimensional way. Perhaps one hundred amino acids have to be

put together in just the right manner to make a protein molecule. Now you have to bring together a collection of protein molecules—maybe two or three hundred—with just the right functions to get a typical living cell. The guidance needed to assemble everything comes from DNA. DNA works hand-in-glove with RNA to direct the correct sequencing of amino acids through biochemical instructions. The making of DNA and RNA would be an even greater problem than creating protein. The synthesis of key building blocks for DNA and RNA has never been successfully done except under highly implausible conditions without any resemblance of those of the early earth.[137]

More than sixty years after Miller and Uery's experiment, many scientists and professors are still touting the results of their experiment as proof of the theory of evolution while being careful not to give out too many details. Highly dramatic statements containing little information are a favorite sport of scientists and professors.

You must be careful not to be impressed by their high-drama, low-information declarations. They still cannot explain in simple terms the *origins* that are critical to the process of evolution. In other words, they can explain at great length how some natural phenomena exist within the evolutionary model, but not how that phenomena originally got there. They explain how life exists and has evolved within the evolutionary model, but not how life got there. The same is true of the second law of thermodynamics (entropy). Its function can be explained, but no one can explain how it came to exist.

The evolutionary model cannot explain the *origin* of the very First Cause in the universe or other simple natural phenomena—the *origin* of biochemical reactions needed at a molecular level for light sensitivity in the human eye, the *origin* of blood clotting, the *origin* of human sexual reproduction, or the *origin* of the mechanisms of human sexual reproduction. These natural phenomena are key to life, yet their *origins* cannot be explained.

Modern cellular research has had a negative impact on the theory of evolution. Today it's a well-known fact that "a single fertilized egg contains chemical instructions that would fill more than five hundred thousand printed pages."[138] "The fertilized egg divides into the 30 trillion cells that make up the human body."[139]

Could all this complexity and information simply have evolved?[140] How could it have even started through evolution? Statistics say, "The probability of a single protein molecule being arranged by chance is 1 in 10^{161}, using all atoms on earth and allowing all the time since the world began."

A minimum set of the required 239 protein molecules for the smallest theoretical life would take $10^{119,841}$ years. That is $10^{119,831}$ times the assumed age of the earth and is a figure with 119,831 zeroes."[140] To put this number into perspective, a trillion billion years has just twenty-one zeros. The universe and earth cannot possibly be old enough for life to have evolved from nothing. There is not enough time in the entire universe for such complexity and information to have realistically developed anywhere purely by chance.

At first glance the theory of evolution seems plausible. Shortly before marrying his first cousin, Darwin spent five years in South America working as a naturalist. He later commented, "I was much struck with certain facts in the distribution of organic beings inhabiting South America ... These facts ... seemed to throw some light on the origin of species ... On my return home, it occurred to me, in 1837, that something might perhaps be made out of this."[141]

Evolution must have been a truly fascinating idea nearly two hundred years ago, before indoor plumbing, the lightbulb, and residential electricity. Such theories simply don't make sense today, especially in light of the dawn of DNA research.

> *Ontogeny recapitulates phylogeny* is the [theory] that in the course of an embryo's development, the embryo repeats the evolutionary history of its species.[142] At various points, an emerging human is a fish, a frog, and finally a fetus. This theory [was] first championed by a German biologist named Ernst Haekel.[143] [Haekel] was charged with fraud by five professors and convicted by a university court at Jena.[144] His forgeries were subsequently made public with the 1911 publication of *Haeckel's Frauds and Forgeries*.[145] There are no redundant vestiges of former evolutionary phases.[146] The DNA for a fetus, frog [or] fish is uniquely programmed for reproduction [only] after its own kind.[147]

Despite new information about fossil records, chemistry, cellular complexity, and DNA research, a Bible was published in 2007 for Christians who believe the theory of evolution! Many proponents for the theory of evolution have insightful ideas about a myriad of subjects related to the topic and they don't mean to mislead anyone. Still, there are some scientists and professors among them who are extremely deliberate and calculating in their attempts to mislead.

The fact is, today's technology is not capable of proving the theory of evolution or the biblical account of creation. Exactly how life got here is still an unsolved mystery. It's obvious that evolution takes place in the world through cross-breeding, genetic mutation, and natural selection. Yet it does not seem possible for evolution to have caused the birth of life. Evolution is a *product* of life. It seems more likely that creation was the original cause of life, because creation is consistent with the intelligent design that is found throughout life on earth and in the universe.

Creation doesn't mean the earth is only six thousand years old. An intelligent design that's consistent with the idea of creation can be found in the Big Bang that was supposedly billions of years ago. Laura Danly, Curator at Griffith Observatory in Los Angeles, explains that,

> If the rate of expansion of the universe right after the big bang had changed by one part in a quintillion, the universe would continue to expand or collapse back on itself and none of this would be possible. That's how precise things had to be for us to be here.[148]

This same extreme precision (intelligent design) can be found in the perfect distribution of matter that had to occur following the Big Bang in order for planets to form and for dozens of Fundamental Constants to instantly come into existence. Hank Hanegraaff points out:

> Though the Big Bang is not taught in the Bible, the theory does lend scientific support to the scriptural teaching that God created the universe *ex nihilo* (out of nothing) ... the Big Bang theory answers

questions concerning the origin of the space-time universe, as opposed to questions concerning the origin of biological life on earth.[149]

How life got here is another story. Modern technology has made it more obvious than ever before that life on earth must have been intelligently designed. Not by a space alien in a petri dish. It is far too complex for that. Hanegraaff concludes:

> When applied to information-rich DNA, irreducibly complex biochemical systems, the Cambrian Explosion in the fossil record, as well as the fact that earth is perfectly situated in the Milky Way for both life and scientific discovery, the existence of an intelligent designer is the most plausible scientific explanation.[150]

It will be a long time before the majority of scientists and professors agree with this statement, but they will come around eventually. Walter Bradley points out that in Darwin's time most still "thought maggots would spontaneously develop from decaying meat" even though hundreds of years earlier, "Francesco Redi demonstrated that meat that was kept away from flies never developed maggots."[151]

Likewise in 1864, five years after the publication of *The Origin of Species* by Charles Darwin, "Louis Pasteur showed that air contains microorganisms that can multiply in water, giving the illusion of the spontaneous generation of life. He announced at the Sorbonne in Paris that 'never will the doctrine of spontaneous generation recover from the mortal blow of this simple experiment.'"[152]

Yet sixty years later in the 1920s, even though "some scientists said they agreed with Pasteur that spontaneous genesis doesn't happen in a short time frame ... they theorized that if you had billions and billions of years—as the late astronomer Carl Sagan liked to say—then it might really happen after all."[153]

It has been 150 years since Pasteur's announcement, yet scientists and professors still believe in spontaneous genesis and the theory of evolution despite evidence to the contrary produced by advancements in science and technology. Even though *The Origin of Species* presents an argument that's not the least bit compelling to modern readers, the theory of evolution described within its antiquated pages is still the most popular choice for those who want a way out of acknowledging the existence of God.

God has never set out to provide you with absolute proof of his existence. It would only make you feel obligated to have a friendship with him. In the beginning God was careful to leave Adam and Eve a way out of having friendships with him and they took it, pursuing knowledge rather than their friendships with God. But not everyone wants a way out. Some people simply take for granted that exaggerations made by scientists and professors about evolution are true. So they assume a friendship with God isn't possible. You don't have to convince them that God exists, just encourage them to try to get to know God for themselves. As they do, the Spirit of God will help them grow.

The important thing for you to know is that there is plenty of evidence to support your Christian faith. The facts play a crucial role in your ability to explain to others why you believe the way you do. You're living in the Information Age. The sum of all human knowledge is now doubling every few years. It is an opportunity for you to be equipped to explain your faith and also to achieve your dream and fulfill your destiny.

More Christian teenagers are alive today than at any other time in history. God is improving the lives of hundreds of millions of teenagers just like you in ways that cannot be achieved through science or government programs. God's plan is to have meaningful friendships with as many people today as possible and to grow the fruit of the Spirit in each one's spirit and personality.

Participating in God's amazing master plan is looked down on in many countries. There are more than 190 countries in the world today and the majority are run by governments that grant citizens very few religious freedoms. Governments such as the United States of America that recognize freedom of religion in writing often censor it in other ways, such as limiting the free exercise of religion in public places. A die is cast by most governments that every citizen is expected to fit into. The goal is that citizens will think alike, act alike, and conform to the mandates of political correctness.

The major religions of the world are similar to these governments because they are exclusive in their claims—meaning they claim to present the only right answers to certain questions and are adamant about establishing limits and defining acceptable behavior. Adherents are expected to voluntarily subject themselves to these restrictions. Ravi Zacharias is an expert on world religions who grew up in India among Hindu, Muslim, Buddhist, and Sikh believers. He is now an award-winning author and international lecturer.

Concerning the exclusive claims of the world's major religions, Zacharias points out that "Muslims believe the sole, sufficient, and consummate miracle of Islam is in the Koran" which is "only recognizable in Arabic" by those who have "a sophisticated knowledge of the language."[154] Buddhists reject "two fundamental assertions of Hinduism—the absolute authority of the Vedas, which are their scriptures, and the caste system."[155] Hinduism "is absolutely uncompromising on three issues: the law of karma ... the authority of the Vedas ... and reincarnation."[156] Sikhism began "as a challenge to both Hinduism and Buddhism."[157] Atheists, without exception, "reject the viewpoints of those who believe in God."[158] "Baha'ism, which is supposed to be a cosmic embrace of all religions, ultimately ends up excluding the exclusivists."[159] New Confucianism asserts that "Confucianism is the highest expression [of] Chinese culture."[160] While "Daoism [is] a countermovement to Confucianism [that] rejects the Confucianist emphasis on rituals, hierarchical social order, and conventional morality."[161]

A die is cast by each of these major religions that everyone is expected to fit into. As with governments, the goal is that adherents will think alike, act alike, and conform to each religion's theological mandates.

In the past hundred years, government controls and mandates that were intended to mold populations into conformity for their own good have instead lead to wars, massacres, and oppressions—resulting in 188 million documented deaths worldwide.[162] The majority of these deaths were not because of religion. They were the direct result of governments fighting for power while often blaming their actions on religions, such as Judaism, Christianity, or Islam.

Like all religions, Christianity is exclusive in its claims. However, Christianity is unique because it features one perfect God (a Holy Trinity) reaching down to humanity and freely giving hope. All other religions consist of rules by which humanity must reach up to God, or a number of gods, and work for hope. Unlike other religions Christianity is also unique because it's comprised of thirty-four thousand different denominations and independent churches worldwide, giving rise to a wide variety of Christians.[163] Such diversity is amazing. But diversity also has its disadvantages, causing Mahatma Gandhi to say, "I like their Christ ... I don't like their Christians."[164]

Ravi Zacharias has said, "I believe that only the answers of Jesus Christ correspond to reality. There is a coherence among his answers unlike those of any other religion."[165] Jesus supports the idea that everyone is different—that your thoughts, emotions, and the expressions of your spirit are entirely unique to you. Scripture says, "When God created mankind, he made them in the likeness of God."[166] The ability to be unique came from God, who gave you this gift so you can achieve the pursuits of your hands, *ordinary and extraordinary*, and have a meaningful friendship with God for a high quality of life and the growth of the church.

Christian churches ought to be places that are uncomplicated and life-affirming. Scripture says, "Religion that God our Father accepts as pure and faultless is this: to look after orphans and widows in their distress."[167] Looking after the less fortunate is a great way to help them see that they're valuable—that their condition does not define their value and the most important thing is what they think, how they feel, and the expressions of their spirit.

Some assert that people who are less fortunate, more than anything else, just need the government to step in and help them out. Offering assistance on such a level forces governments to mandate terms by which assistance will or won't be given, as well as who will pay for it and how. The most important consideration then becomes society and who controls it, not the need of each individual citizen.

All of humanity shares this same need and weakness—the need for a civil society and a weakness for power. The human race is skilled at governing, but the governments it creates are often more interested in exercising political power than addressing humanity's need for a civil society. That would require a dream. Only a dream can produce a civil society that demonstrates the ability to resist power. The dream of a civil society ought to be freedom—as much freedom as possible for every citizen.

God loves freedom. The first three words God ever spoke to humanity following creation were, "You are free."[168] Did you know that? Scripture encourages everyone to "live as free people."[169] You're also encouraged to "approach God with freedom."[170] You ought to be free. Even Satan is free—that's how important freedom is to God. Few facts are clear about Satan. But one fact you can know for sure is that Satan is free to roam the earth, to torment people, to lead them astray, and even to masquerade as an angel of light.

Satan was not created wicked, but was free to choose. Scripture says, "Even the archangel Michael, when he was disputing with the devil … did not himself dare to condemn him for slander but said, 'The Lord rebuke you!'"[171] The archangel Michael respected the freedom of Satan. Yet in the very next verse you're told in scripture that "people slander whatever they do not understand."[172]

Most governments simply don't understand the value of freedom. Instead to maintain government's control over society they have silenced certain citizens because of their ideas and spiritual expressions—demonstrating that the individual's freedom and quality of life is not important. A great many people will never experience real freedom. However, you can always be completely free in spirit. Jesus said himself that "if the Son sets you free, you will be free indeed."[173]

No government can stop you from personally asking God to accept Jesus's punishment and separation in place of your own. It's an act of one person—with their thoughts, emotions, and spirit—speaking to one God (Father, Son, and Spirit) in the ultimate expression of an individual's value and freedom. You don't even have to know all the details, as explained in *Teenagers Leave a Mark*. A simple prayer is sufficient, such as, "I'm imperfect; forgiven me! The world is dark and dangerous; help me! Life is exciting and wonderful; lead me!" God will take it from there. It's an act that only you and God can be certain of, and it becomes apparent to those around you through your newfound character traits, including the fruit of the Spirit.

Governments have always come and gone. None of them have lasted nearly as long as Christianity. They can be unstable and overbearing at times, but governments can still be helpful, and you want to have a healthy society and be a good citizen. You can contribute so much more to society by participating in God's amazing master plan. Join a church where you can express your beliefs in ways that show compassion and emphasize the inherent value of every individual. It's one of the most patriotic things you can do for your country.

Most governments want citizens to be dependent upon them instead of being dependent upon one another. But people need friendships and it isn't possible to have friendships with governments. Even though governments can provide all the basic necessities, they can never be trusted to care for a person as an individual. Still, governments crave power and want to be involved in each citizen's life. It's hard to be happy and develop the fruit of the Spirit when an impersonal government is way too involved in your life. If you distrust your own government, or even scientists and professors, that distrust can lead to feelings of unhappiness, insecurity, and animosity, which are taxing on your emotions.

When you lose control of your emotions, you lose control of your life. Only the fruit of the Spirit which is masterfully grown over time by the Spirit of God in your own spirit and personality can deliver the love, joy, peace, patience, kindness, goodness, faithfulness, gentleness, and self-control you seek. That enables you to better control your own emotions so you can feel more stable and secure in life.

Steven Covey has observed in his book *Smart Trust* that today there is "a literal crisis of trust in most of the world—in our societies, our institutions, our governments, our media, our health care services, our organizations, our relationships, and even our personal lives. In some cases trust has never been lower than it is today."[174] Covey calls it a crisis because we need to be able to trust. He points out that "trust is directly linked to the degree of prosperity, energy, and joy we experience" in life.[175]

Scripture encourages you by saying, "May the God of hope fill you with all joy and peace as you trust in him."[176] As you place your trust in God, you will discover for yourself that God *can* be trusted—not for a perfect life, but for joy and peace in life. God is your most stable companion. Loved ones are lost when they die and friendships in life are sometimes destroyed. But scripture says God "will never leave you nor forsake you."[177] With God's help you don't have to strive for so much control in life. Instead your trust in God will produce *self*-control and a real sense of security.

Placing your trust in God and his amazing master plan is the final component to a balanced approach to life. You're embracing your strengths and weaknesses, pursuing your goals and dream (ordinary and extraordinary pursuits), expressing who you are at your core, having a meaningful friendship with God for your own quality of life and the growth of the church, and experiencing the fruit of the Spirit being grown over time by the Spirit of God in your own spirit and personality. This balanced approach to life helps God achieve his own dream as he gives to you more and more. The same goes for Jesus as he saves you and the Spirit of God as he engages you.

God knows what you're capable of and he believes in you enough to challenge you to live a balanced life. If you trust God too, then you absolutely must speak with others about life and God. If not, you will eventually look back over your own life and wonder what might have happened in God's plan if you would have spoken with others more often. You may not realize how much those around you are searching or hurting, and you probably underestimate how much you can help.

It can seem like such a mystery when you wonder what will happen if you do speak up. But that's a good thing. Everyone seeks excitement in life and here it is. You need more mystery in your life. Not the kind of uncertainty that causes you stress. You need the kind of mystery that comes from the unexplained ... something that arouses your curiosity—a puzzling story with an obscure plot that entices you to speculate about what the secret is and what will happen next. As you wonder what will happen, you will sense the Spirit of God encouraging you to embrace the moment.

As you place your trust in God and try to enjoy the mystery, you will want to speak more often. This is because you will get the chance to observe the character of God in action through the lives of others and grow to understand truths about God that may have otherwise remained beyond your understanding.

Three figures in scripture are famous for having embraced the mystery of speaking with others about God. They are Daniel, Paul, and John. None of them knew what would happen if they decided to speak. Each of them had to make a conscious decision to embrace the mystery—to take an interest in the unexplained, to be curious and speculate about what would happen. Fortunately they decided to speak. In doing so they were able to leave a mark on others, observe the character of God in action, and understand truths about God that had previously been unknown.

You have the same opportunity. At any given moment there may be someone nearby who is hurting or searching. Whether it's a family member, friend, or someone you just met, you can learn from Daniel, Paul, and John how to embrace the mystery and speak with them about God.

The mystery of speaking with others about God was first mentioned in scripture in 604 BC when Nebuchadnezzar, king of Babylon, had a disturbing dream about future events. He kept the dream a secret as he summoned his magicians, fortune tellers, and astrologers. Then he told them, "I have had a dream that troubles me and I want to know what it means ... tell me the dream, and I will know that you can interpret it."[178] Even though the Babylonian empire was vast, no one could be found to tell him the dream.

Upon learning that the king intended to put to death all of his wise men, a Jewish captive named Daniel—one of the king's wise men himself—went to the king and "asked for time, so that he might interpret the dream for him. Then Daniel returned to his house and explained the matter to his friends Hananiah, Mishael and Azariah. He urged them to plead for mercy from the God of heaven concerning this mystery."[179] That night "the mystery was revealed to Daniel in a vision."[180] Since Daniel was able to describe the dream and explain its interpretation, Nebuchadnezzar declared, "Your God is the God of gods and the Lord of kings and a revealer of mysteries."[181]

After speaking with the king Daniel explained, "This mystery has been revealed to me, not because I have greater wisdom than anyone else alive, but so ... you may understand."[182] There are teenagers around you who are just as troubled as Nebuchadnezzar. You need to be willing to embrace the mystery and speak with them. Not to show how wise you are, but to help them gain a better understanding of God. Pray about it first and ask friends to pray with you. It's a great way to build trust that the Spirit of God will help you speak the right words at the right moment.

During AD 5 in the Roman Empire, "Saul, who was also called Paul" was born to a predominant Jewish family.[183] He grew to become a high-ranking Pharisee who was passionate about destroying the early church. But an amazing change occurred in his life when he was in Damascus overseeing the imprisonment of Christians. Saul unexpectedly experienced his own conversion to Christianity.

Then according to Saul he simply left town for a while. He said, "I did not go up to Jerusalem to see those who were apostles before I was, but I went into Arabia. Later I returned to Damascus."[184] Saul must have needed time to think. He may have struggled with what to say to people after his conversion. However, when he returned from Arabia he was ready to speak. "Those who heard him were astonished and asked, 'Isn't he the man who raised havoc in Jerusalem ... and hasn't he come here to take [us] as prisoners to the chief priests?'"[185] Despite how strange it was, Saul still continued to speak and "grew more and more powerful and baffled the Jews living in Damascus by proving that Jesus is the Messiah."[186]

Three years later Saul mustered the courage to travel to Jerusalem and speak with the leaders of the church there. Scripture says:

> When he came to Jerusalem, he tried to join the disciples, but they were all afraid of him, not believing that he really was a disciple. But Barnabas

took him and brought him to the apostles. He told them how Saul on his journey had seen the Lord and that the Lord had spoken to him, and how in Damascus he had preached fearlessly in the name of Jesus.[187]

Throughout his life it was a struggle for Saul to speak. Even in Jerusalem among his own people, "he talked and debated with the Hellenistic Jews, but they tried to kill him."[188] Afterward he began to address himself as Paul, the Latin name he bore as a Roman citizen. Apparently he thought changing his name might help.

Despite the constant struggle, for three decades Paul traveled throughout Asia Minor and Europe, encouraging Christians and establishing churches. Like Paul, you may struggle at first to speak with people about God, even if you easily share your opinions on other matters. You might need a little time to gather your thoughts before you're ready to begin. But God needs you to begin speaking and to continue speaking.

Having been a bully himself, Paul understood that people are bullies. Comparing himself to most Christians, Paul said, "I have … been in prison more frequently, been flogged more severely, and been exposed to death again and again."[189] Whenever you speak with people, you run the risk of being bullied. Bullies are prepared to do or say anything to get the response they want out of you. If you shrink back, then they have succeeded. On the other hand, if you get an attitude about it you will seem to be just as aggressive as they are. Simply say what you have to say and do not be offended by how they respond, even the people you're closest to. Their responses may hurt your feelings or even break your heart. Still, be willing to put your heart on the line; be polite and allow them to respond. It's a necessary process that can hurt a little, but you'll discover that it will help them grow over time.

Don't worry if they make a dramatic statement such as "A loving God cannot exist with so much pain and suffering in the world." You can be sure they're playing you. They understand that people cannot know happiness without knowing pain and suffering. They're just playing as if they don't understand. It's easy to understand that God was *not* created and everyone else was. Before anyone was created there was only God—so no one else is uncreated and perfect like God. Adam and Eve experienced perfection in the Garden of Eden. However, since they didn't know any different they didn't appreciate what they had. They craved knowledge and eventually gave up their microcosm of perfection in order to know the truth about everything in life. As a result today you get to know it all—happiness as well as pain and suffering.

Your life and God's are not so different. Charles Dickens began *A Tale of Two Cities* by explaining, "It was the best of times, it was the worst of times ..." That's how life is: some of the best and worst all mixed together. Life is the same for God. The angels messed up, people messed up, and now nature is messed up. So God isn't lounging around in a state of bliss. His life is more complicated than yours. But God didn't mess up—none of these messes were unexpected and nothing went wrong for God.

Everything is simply free to run its own imperfect course and this freedom is a loving gift from God. Even Satan was free to turn on God and convince others to do the same. In the process he caused angels to be kicked out of heaven, people to be cut off from God, and creation to be corrupted. Yet he whispers in your ear, "The world is messed up. Don't you agree that it's all God's fault?" While God whispers, "Don't believe every idea that pops into your head.

Won't you put your trust in me and my amazing master plan?" As you contemplate these two ideas, regardless of which idea you adopt as your own, you will still continue to experience the best and worst of times mixed together.

Even Jesus experienced the best and worst of times. So he's a great example, because he handled it perfectly. God created you to be able to handle life the same way. So embrace the fact that you cannot know happiness without pain and suffering, and that the best and worst of times are all mixed together. Don't push God away because of it—embrace it as something you and God have in common, and seek God's help. If you ask God, he will help you handle it perfectly!

As knowledge continues to increase, the worst of times will grow worse while the best of times will grow even better, and all of it will culminate at the end of time. Don't let that bother you. Embrace the fact that they will increase simultaneously, knowing that everything is free to run its course. Meanwhile, you will continue experiencing happiness as well as pain and suffering, but you will grow to handle it better than you do today. These are simple ideas that anyone can understand. If someone tells you they cannot believe in a loving God because there is pain and suffering in the world, they're just playing you.

In AD 95 John was exiled on the Greek island of Patmos because of anti-Christian persecution within the Roman Empire. While in exile at the age of ninety-two he was unexpectedly recruited to be the author of what would later become the last book of the Bible. John explained, "I heard behind me a loud voice like a trumpet, which said: 'Write on a scroll what you see and send it to the seven churches.'"[190]

John began seeing amazing visions that became the book of Revelation. He had no idea what would come of the book. All he knew for sure was that he wouldn't live to see the mark the book would leave on others. But he communicated what he was given anyway. As with John, there will be times when the opportunity to speak with others will sneak up on you. Even though you might be caught off-guard and you may never get a chance to see what will come of it later, God still needs you to embrace the mystery and speak.

Daniel, Paul, and John revealed mysteries about God's amazing master plan. Yet no matter how amazing these mysteries were, the greatest mystery for each of them was what would happen if they spoke up. They truly had no idea and must have wondered, especially considering each one's circumstances. But each of them chose to embrace the mystery anyway. All three had life-changing experiences as a result.

Daniel got to witness the rise and fall of Babylon firsthand, as well as King Nebuchadnezzar's religious conversion. By interpreting dreams and visions Daniel also got to gaze into the future at the Roman Empire and beyond it to the last great empire. He learned that the Roman Empire would eventually fall and afterward no nation would ever again be as capable of ruling with such an iron fist.

Daniel also foresaw the last great kingdom that is yet to arise. It "will have some of the strength" of the Roman Empire.[191] Yet the ten nations comprising it will be "partly strong and partly brittle" and "the people will be a mixture and will not remain united."[192] Like all the kingdoms before it, this last great empire will fall and the kingdom of God will finally be established on earth. Daniel would never have experienced such foresight and adventure if he hadn't been willing to speak. He probably would have led a good life, but it wouldn't have been nearly as interesting.

Paul got to see new places and meet new people—governors and kings. Some believe he even met Caesar. These were opportunities for Paul to explain and defend the faith he felt so passionate about. His willingness to speak is what enabled him to build countless friendships as he traveled to twenty-eight cities in three countries. Paul founded fourteen churches and later wrote letters to them, which eventually became thirteen books of the Bible. Paul was personally associated with a hundred other people in the Bible, including dozens of colleagues and friends whom he mentioned by name in scripture. These friendships were created because of Paul's willingness to speak in spite of the fact that it was a constant struggle.

Unlike Paul, John did not get to speak with many people in person. But his willingness to communicate through writing gained him the opportunity to see a vision of the end of everything. He got to foresee a day when "there will be no more delay" and "the mystery of God will be accomplished."[193] At a time of political unrest, during an age in which soldiers were storming Jerusalem, burning the temple, and leaving the city in ruins, John witnessed a mystery of God—that the way life was in his day was not the way it would always be. Jesus told him "I, Jesus, have sent my angel to give you this testimony for the churches."[194]

John was given a rare opportunity to encourage people in the churches. When he wrote to them he said:

> I saw the Holy City, the new Jerusalem ... and I
> heard a loud voice from the throne saying, "Look!
> God's dwelling place is now among the people, and
> he will dwell with them. They will be his people,
> and God himself will be with them and be their

God. He will wipe every tear from their eyes. There will be no more death or mourning or crying or pain, for the old order of things has passed away."[195]

Just as with Daniel, Paul, and John, you can expect great results when you speak, especially if you're careful about what you say and how you say it. You don't know what will happen any more than they did before they spoke. But you can be sure that, just as with them, you will definitely lead a more interesting life, build new friendships, make existing friendships more meaningful, gain insights into God's character, and know that good things will eventually come from the marks you leave on others through your willingness to communicate with them.

Remember that it's okay to be afraid to speak. Speaking with others about God threatens to change both you and the person you're speaking with into better people, the likes of which neither of you have experienced before. So be afraid, but be brave. Grab the bull by the horns and go for it—you will be glad you did. You will be taking a bigger risk if you don't find the courage to speak up. You definitely risk losing out on a lot. It's less of a risk just to say something and see how it goes.

Keep in mind that these conversations often turn out perfectly. It's a real possibility. You don't have to speak perfectly, be skilled at using the power of your personality, or even be convincing. You just need to speak honestly from a balanced approach to life. Pause for a moment and remind yourself before you speak that "I'm not alone in this conversation. There's a dynamic third person in the conversation with me whose dream is to engage the person I'll be speaking with." The Spirit of God is always present, helping you leave a mark on others that will turn out perfectly in the end.

Many people simply never think about God. He never even crosses their minds, so someone else has to bring up the subject. Don't rob them of a great opportunity! If you're thinking about God, you ought to say so and encourage them to do the same. It's not complicated. You just need to be friendly and complimentary, and speak in a way that is comfortable and appropriate for you. Then you can ask the person you're speaking with to share his or her own thoughts. Listen and learn about where that person is in his or her own discovery of God.

Whether in social settings or chance meetings throughout the day, you bring up so many inane subjects to talk about. Why not speak about God or about calling on God? That's what life comes down to: calling on God. This one-on-one interaction is the most beautiful and meaningful part of life. Everyone needs to experience it. You can feel confident about encouraging and challenging others to do it. You can even help them. An effective way to speak with others about God is to pray with them about whatever is concerning them at that moment. Just say, "Let's pray about it." Then lead them in a heartfelt prayer. It's that easy! Afterward you can suggest they take time more often to call on God on their own.

Encouraging others to call on God is easy to do when you know who God is and what his dream is. You know the person you're asking other people to call on and why they need God in their lives. You know that when God gave them the ability to be unique, he did so hoping they would call on him and begin a friendship with him. God gave them needs and weaknesses so they would need to call on him. He wants them to pursue a dream so they'll have a positive reason to call on him. That stretches their character so they can deeply call on him. Then their character grows as a reward for calling on him. You know that Jesus will save them so they can call on God, the Spirit of God will engage them and help them call on God, and the church is a great place for them to call on God with like-minded people. So you can feel really good about speaking with other teenagers and encouraging them to call on God.

God's amazing master plan involves the Savior, the Spirit of God, and the church. Also, whenever the mystery of his plan is revealed, it always involves a person who is willing to speak. This scenario hasn't changed. Whenever you speak with others, you leave a mark and witness the mystery of God's plan unfolding. If the majority of Christian teenagers made speaking with other teenagers a priority, the church would quickly become a driving force that represents the wisdom of God in the world today.

Nothing can stop you from leaving a mark. No matter what the circumstances, you're free to embrace your strengths and weaknesses, to pursue your goals and dream (ordinary and extraordinary pursuits), to express who you are at your core, and to have a meaningful friendship with God for your own quality of life and for the growth of the church, while experiencing the fruit of the Spirit being grown over time in your own spirit and personality. Politics, economics, and religion will always influence your world. But regardless of what is happening politically, economically, or within the world's major religions, you're always free to leave a mark and to speak with people about God.

Make sure you leave a mark as you pursue your dream. You can call your dream whatever you like. Call it a vision for your life, God's plan, or a calling. As you know, it can be in any area of your life, as long as it comes from a predominant need or weakness. But don't try to change that need or weakness yourself. Instead focus on your dream, and while you're doing one task in order to achieve your dream the Spirit of God will help you grow. It's the same whether you're a strong person or whether you're acutely aware of your need or weakness. Destinies and dreams put all teenagers on the same level.

Remember that it's best to pursue a handful of dreams at a time: a lifelong dream for the long-term, one or more personal dreams for direction in life, and an urgent dream if a crisis arises. The question is, are you willing to pursue at least one dream? Even if it's really challenging and stretches your character? Will you do it if it brings you happiness and a richness to life, and brings you closer to God? What if it enables God to reveal his power in your life and enables you to play a role in a master plan that only God knows? There is a reason why your destiny is what it is. You must believe that. God has a plan and it involves your dream.

Are you willing to receive from God? His dream is to give to you! God has a plan to change the world and grow the church while at the same time producing the fruit of the Spirit in your life. But you need to place your trust in him and allow the Spirit of God to help you grow. Otherwise you won't enjoy your own life or be able to help other teenagers enjoy theirs.

Remarkable things will happen when you embrace the mystery of speaking with other teenagers about God. If you care about them, challenge them to become the people they really want to be. You might upset them at first. But it's one of the most caring and thoughtful things you can ever do. If you make speaking with other teenagers a priority, the church will be one step closer to becoming a driving force that represents the wisdom of God in the world—that's God's plan. Are you ready to participate in God's amazing master plan?

Notes

PREFACE—You Have An Amazing Spirit

[1]   *Holy Bible: King James Version* (Michigan: Zondervan Pub. 1984 by The Zondervan Corporation) Ephesians 2:5.
[2]   *NIV,* Romans 15:13.
[3]   *NIV,* Romans 15:4.
[4]   *NIV,* II Corinthians 12:9.
[5]   *NIV,* II Corinthians 12:9–10.
[6]   *NIV,* Hebrews 4:15.
[7]   *NIV,* Romans 8:26.

INTRODUCTION—Preparing For A Dream

[8]   Martin Luther King Jr., *Encyclopedia Britannica, Inc.* (Encyclopedia Britannica 1994–2001).
[9]   *Quotes and Quips* (Salt Lake City, Utah: Franklin Covey Co. 84119 1996, 1998).

CHAPTER 1—Discover Your Purpose

[10]   *NIV,* Genesis 5:1.

CHAPTER 2—Define Your Destiny

[11]   Rick Warren, *The Purpose-Driven Life* (Michigan: Zondervan Pub. 2002 by Rick Warren), 273–274.
[12]   *NIV,* Exodus 4:10.
[13]   *NIV,* Judges 6:15.
[14]   *NIV,* Joshua 2:11.
[15]   *NIV,* Hebrews 11:34.

CHAPTER 3—Design Your Dream

16   *NIV,* John 17:24.
17   *NIV,* Mathew 17:2–3.
18   John Whitmore, *Coaching for Performance* (Nicholas Brealey Pub. 1992, 1993, 1994, 1996, 2002 by John Whitmore).
19   *Quotes and Quips* (Salt Lake City, Utah: Franklin Covey Co. 84119 1996, 1998).
20   Mark Twain, *Mark Twain's Notebook* (1898).
21   *NIV,* John 17:1.
22   *NIV,* Hebrews 12:2.
23   *The Saturday Evening Post*; Quoted by G.S. Viereck in the article, "What Life Means to Einstein"; October 29,1929.
24   *NIV,* Ecclesiastes 2:26.

CHAPTER 4—Who Says It's Not Possible?

25   *NIV,* John 4:23.
26   *NIV,* Romans 8:2.
27   *Science, Philosophy and Religion, A Symposium*; published by the Conference on Science, Philosophy and Religion in Their Relation to the Democratic Way of Life, Inc. 1941 (New York).
28   Albert Einstein, *Out of My Later Years* (Open Road Media 2011).
29   *NIV,* Philippians 4:8 (emphasis added).

CHAPTER 5—Now You've Done It!

30   *NIV,* Hebrews 11:1–2.
31   *Harper's Monthly Magazine*; Quoted by M.A. Rosanoff; September 1932.
32   *NIV,* Hebrews 4:15–16.
33   *Webster's New World Dictionary;* Second College Edition (New York: Princeton-Hall Simon and Schuster 1970, 1972, 1974, 1976, 1978, 1979, 1980 by Simon and Schuster).
34   *NIV,* I Corinthians 1:27, 29.
35   *NIV,* Philippians 4:6–7.

CHAPTER 6—Hope Changes Everything

36   Jürgen Moltmann, *The Experiment Hope* (Philadelphia: Fortress Press 1975 by Fortress Press).

37 *NIV,* John 20:19.
38 *NIV,* John 21:3.
39 *NIV,* Romans 8:16.
40 *NIV,* 2 Corinthians 5:5.
41 *NIV,* Hebrews 6:19.
42 Gavin de Becker, *The Gift of Fear* (New York: Dell Publishing 1997 by Gavin de Becker) 75.
43 de Becker, *The Gift of Fear,* 73.
44 de Becker, *The Gift of Fear,* 73.
45 *NIV,* Romans 7:18.
46 *NIV,* Romans 15:13.
47 *NIV,* Romans 15:4.
48 *NIV,* John 14:16–17.
49 *NIV,* John 14:26.
50 *The Age of Reason* (London: Barrios, Sold by D. I. Eaton; 1794, 1795, 1807) brackets added.
51 *The Age of Reason.*
52 *NIV,* John 16:32.
53 *NIV,* Matthew 6:6.
54 *NIV,* Psalm 46:10.
55 *NIV,* Romans 5:5.
56 Robert Kent "Bobby" Brewer, *Christian Research Journal,* volume 25, number 2 (North Carolina: Christian Research Institute 2002 by the Christian Research Institute).
57 Francis A Schaeffer, *The God Who Is There* (Illinois: InterVarsity Press 1968 by L'Abri Fellowship).

CHAPTER 7—Confidence, Compassion, And Conflict

58 Leigh Buchanan, *Inc Magazine;* February 1, 2003 Issue (Mansueto Ventures LLC).
59 *NIV,* Hebrews 4:16.
60 *NIV,* John 11: 41–42.
61 *NIV,* I John 5:14–15.
62 *Hebrew Dictionary* (Babylon.com 1997–2011 Babylon Ltd.).
63 *NIV,* Genesis 3:7.
64 *NIV,* Genesis 3:21.
65 *NIV,* James 5:11.
66 *NIV,* Job 42:3.

67   *NIV,* Job 42:6.

68   *NIV,* Job 42:10.

69   *NIV,* Job 42:12.

70   *NIV,* Job 42:5.

71   *NIV,* Philippians 1:6.

72   *NIV,* John 11:41–42 (emphasis added).

73   Leigh Buchanan, *Inc Magazine;* February 1, 2003 Issue (Mansueto Ventures LLC).

CHAPTER 8—Don't Look Now, But You're In The Lead!

74   *Get Motivated!,* Speaker Outlines (Get Motivated Seminars, Inc. 2003) 112.

75   *Get Motivated!,* Speaker Outlines, 112.

76   *Quotes and Quips* (Salt Lake City, Utah: Franklin Covey Co. 84119 1996, 1998).

77   *NIV,* Matthew 27:46.

78   *NIV,* Hebrews 5:7–9.

79   Rev. Andrew A. Bonar, *Memoir and Remains of the Rev. R. M. McCheyne* (published by William Middleton, 1846) 243.

80   *NIV,* I Peter 2:9.

81   *NIV,* Jeremiah 29:11.

82   "Eleanor Roosevelt Quotes" (Copyright 2001 – 2013 BrainyQuote) http://www.brainyquote.com/quotes/quotes/e/eleanorroo100940.html.

CHAPTER 9—Expressing Who You Are At Your Core

83   *NIV,* Ecclesiastes 3:12.

84   *NIV,* Hebrews 10:19.

85   *NIV,* Hebrews 6:19.

86   *NIV,* Hebrews 10:21–22.

87   *NIV,* Matthew 6:32–33.

88   *NIV,* Romans 14:17.

89   "Crime in the United States; International Comparison; Homicide," last modified on August 2, 2011, http://en.wikipedia.org/wiki/Crime_in_the_United_States (WikiPedia).

90   *NIV,* Exodus 34:14.

91   Richard Newman, *African American Quotations* (Oryx Press) 64.

92   "Malcolm Forbes Quotes" (Copyright 2001 – 2014 BrainyQuote)

93 *NIV,* I John 4:7–8.
94 *NIV,* Genesis 3:8.
95 *NIV,* I Corinthians 13:8.
96 *NIV,* I Corinthians 13:13.
97 C.S. Lewis, *Mere Christianity* (New York: Collier Books; Macmillan Publishing C. 1943, 1945, 1952 by Macmillan Publishing Co.) 74.
98 Lewis, *Mere Christianity,* 74.
99 Hank Hanegraaff, *The Bible Answer Book* (Nashville, Tennessee: Thomas Nelson Book Group 2004 by Hank Hanegraaff) 141.
100 *NIV,* I Corinthians 13:13.
101 *Christian History: Thomas Aquinas,* Magazine Number 73 (Illinois: Christianity Today International 2002)
102 *Christian History: Thomas Aquinas,* Magazine Number 73
103 *NIV,* Ecclesiastes 5:19–20.
104 *NIV,* Romans 8:6.

CHAPTER 10—God's Amazing Master Plan

105 *Webster's New World Dictionary;* Second College Edition (New York: Princeton-Hall Simon and Schuster 1970, 1972, 1974, 1976, 1978, 1979, 1980 by Simon and Schuster).
106 *Webster's New World Dictionary;* Second College Edition
107 *NIV,* Acts 1:6.
108 *NIV,* Acts 1:7–8.
109 *NIV,* Acts 1:8.
110 *NIV,* Genesis 1:1–2.
111 *NIV,* Luke 1:35.
112 *NIV,* Luke 3:21–22.
113 *NIV,* Acts 2:2–4.
114 *NIV,* Acts 10:44.
115 *NIV,* John 3:6.
116 *NIV,* John 3:7.
117 *NIV,* Matthew 18:3.
118 *NIV,* Hebrews 1:12 (brackets added).
119 *NIV,* Ephesians 1:11.
120 *NIV,* Ephesians 3:10.
121 *NIV,* Ephesians 5:25–27.
122 *NIV,* Galatians 5:22.

123   Hank Hanegraaff, *Fatal Flaws* (Nashville Tennessee: W Publishing Group; Thomas Nelson 2003 by Hank Hanegraaff) 18.

124   Henry M. Morris and Gary E. Parker, *What Is Creation Science?* Revised Edition (El Cajon, California: Master Books 1987) 138.

125   Duane T. Gish, *Evolution: The Fossils Still Say No!* (El Cajon, California 1995 by Institute For Creation Research) 344–347.

126   Gish, *Evolution: The Fossils Still Say No!* (brackets added) 344–347.

127   Gish, *Evolution: The Fossils Still Say No!* (brackets added) 280.

128   Gish, *Evolution: The Fossils Still Say No!* (brackets added) 280.

129   Hank Hanegraaff, *Fatal Flaws* (Nashville Tennessee: W Publishing Group; Thomas Nelson 2003 by Hank Hanegraaff) 34.

130   Hanegraaff, *Fatal Flaws,* 35.

131   Ina T. Taylor, *In The Minds of Men*, 3rd Edition; (Toronto: TFE Publishing 1991) 237.

132   Taylor, *In The Minds of Men*, 3rd Edition, 240.

133   Lee Strobel, *The Case For Faith* (Michigan: Zondervan Pub. 2000 by Lee Strobel) 96 (brackets added).

134   Strobel, *The Case For Faith*, 96.

135   Strobel, *The Case For Faith*, 97.

136   Strobel, *The Case For Faith*, 99.

137   Strobel, *The Case For Faith*, 98–100 (brackets added).

138   A. E. Wilder-Smith, *The Natural Sciences Know Nothing of Evolution* (Costa Mesa, California: T.W.F.T. Publishers 1981) 82.

139   A. E. Wilder-Smith, *The Origin of Life*, episode 3, videotape (Gilbert Arizona: Produced by Eden in 1983).

140   James F. Coppedge, *Evolution: Possible or Impossible?* (Northridge California: Probability Research In Molecular Biology 1993) 110, 114.

141   Charles Darwin, *The Origin of Species*, 1998 Modern Library Paperback Edition (New York: The Modern Library 1993 by Random House Inc.) 18.

142   William R Fix, *The Bone Peddlers: Selling Evolution* (New York: Macmillan 1984) 285 (brackets added).

143   Hank Hanegraaff, *Fatal Flaws* (Nashville Tennessee: W Publishing Group; Thomas Nelson 2003 by Hank Hanegraaff) 69 (brackets added).

144   *In The Beginning: Compelling Evidence for Creation and the Flood*, 6th Edition; by Walt Brown; 1995 by Center For Scientific Creation; Phoenix (brackets added)

145   Assmusth and Hall, *Haeckel's Frauds and Forgeries* (Bombay Press 1911).

146 Henry M. Morrison, *Scientific Creationism*, public school edition (San Diego: C.L.P. Publishers 1981) 77.

147 Morrison, *Scientific Creationism*, 75–78.

148 Laura Danly, *The Universe: God and the Universe*, season 6, episode 7 (A&E Television Networks, L.L.C. 2011).

149 Hank Hanegraaff, *The Bible Answer Book* (Nashville, Tennessee: Thomas Nelson Book Group 2004 by Hank Hanegraaff) 366–367.

150 Hank Hanegraaff, *The Bible Answer Book* (Nashville, Tennessee: Thomas Nelson Book Group 2004 by Hank Hanegraaff) 389.

151 Lee Strobel, *The Case For Faith* (Michigan: Zondervan Pub. 2000 by Lee Strobel) 95.

152 Strobel, *The Case For Faith*, 95.

153 Strobel, *The Case For Faith*, 95.

154 Strobel, *The Case For Faith*, 149.

155 Strobel, *The Case For Faith*, 149.

156 Strobel, *The Case For Faith*, 149.

157 Strobel, *The Case For Faith*, 149.

158 Strobel, *The Case For Faith*, 149.

159 Strobel, *The Case For Faith*, 149.

160 "New Confucianism," last modified on 27 July 2014 at 20:07, http://en.wikipedia.org/wiki/New_Confucianism (Wikipedia is a registered trademark of the Wikimedia Foundation, Inc.) brackets added.

161 "Taoism," last modified on 18 September 2014 at 13:30, http://en.wikipedia.org/wiki/Taoism (Wikipedia is a registered trademark of the Wikimedia Foundation, Inc.) brackets added.

162 Matthew White, *Historical Atlas of the Twentieth Century*, last modified 25 March 2003, http://users.erols.com/mwhite28/20centry.htm (1998–2001 by Matthew White)

163 *World Christian Encyclopedia*: A comparative survey of churches and religions—AD 30 to 2200 (Oxford University Press 2001).

164 Lee Strobel, *The Case For Faith* (Michigan: Zondervan Pub. 2000 by Lee Strobel) 150.

165 Strobel, *The Case For Faith*, 151.

166 *NIV*, Genesis 5:1.

167 *NIV*, James 1:27.

168 *NIV*, Genesis 2:16.

169 *NIV*, 1 Peter 2:16.

170 *NIV*, Ephesians 3:12.

171 *NIV*, Jude 1:9.

172 *NIV,* Jude 1:10.

173 *NIV,* John 8:36.

174 Stephen Covey and Greg Link, *Smart Trust* (Free Press. A division of Simon & Schuster, Inc. 2012 by Coveylink, LLC) 10.

175 Covey and Link, *Smart Trust,* 25.

176 *NIV,* Romans 15:13.

177 *NIV,* Deuteronomy 31:6.

178 *NIV,* Daniel 2:3–9.

179 *NIV,* Daniel 2:16–18.

180 *NIV,* Daniel 2:19.

181 *NIV,* Daniel 2:47.

182 *NIV,* Daniel 2:30.

183 *NIV,* Acts 13:9.

184 *NIV,* Galatians 1:17.

185 *NIV,* Acts 9:21 (brackets added).

186 *NIV,* Acts 9:22.

187 *NIV,* Acts 9:26–27.

188 *NIV,* Acts 9:29.

189 *NIV,* II Corinthians 11:23.

190 *NIV,* Revelation 1:11.

191 *NIV,* Daniel 2:41.

192 *NIV,* Daniel 2:42–43.

193 *NIV,* Revelation 10:6–7.

194 *NIV,* Revelation 22:16.

195 *NIV,* Revelation 21:2–4.